Was Blind, But Now I See

Critical America

GENERAL EDITORS:
RICHARD DELGADO AND JEAN STEFANCIC

To Be an American:
Cultural Pluralism and the Rhetoric of Assimilation
BILL ONG HING

Negrophobia and Reasonable Racism:
The Hidden Costs of Being Black in America
JODY DAVID ARMOUR

Black and Brown in America:
The Case for Cooperation
BILL PIATT

Black Rage Confronts the Law
PAUL HARRIS

Selling Words: Free Speech in a Commercial Culture
R. GEORGE WRIGHT

The Color of Crime:
Racial Hoaxes, White Fear, Black Protectionism, Police
Harassment, and Other Macroaggressions
KATHERYN K. RUSSELL

The Smart Culture: Society, Intelligence, and Law
ROBERT L. HAYMAN, JR.

Was Blind, But Now I See: White Race Consciousness and the Law
BARBARA J. FLAGG

Was Blind,
But Now I See

White Race Consciousness & the Law

BARBARA J. FLAGG

NEW YORK UNIVERSITY PRESS
New York and London

NEW YORK UNIVERSITY PRESS
New York and London

Library of Congress Cataloging-in-Publication Data
Flagg, Barbara J., 1947–
Was blind, but now I see : white race consciousness and the law /
Barbara J. Flagg.
p. cm.
Includes index.
ISBN 0-8147-2643-7 (cloth : alk. paper)
1. Afro-Americans—Legal status, laws, etc. 2. Race
discrimination—Law and legislation—United States. 3. United
States—Race relations. I. Title.
KF4757.F59 1998
346.7301′3—dc21   97-21162
                          CIP

Manufactured in the United States of America

10 9 8 7 6 5 4 3 2 1

To my mentors

Ruth Bader Ginsburg
Herma Hill Kay

Amazing grace! How sweet the sound,
That saved a wretch like me!
I once was lost, but now am found,
Was blind, but now I see.

—*John Newton*

John Newton (1725–1807) was captain of a slave ship from 1750 to 1754, but a religious conversion gradually led him to repudiate his former occupation and eventually to write an antislavery pamphlet titled "Thoughts upon the African Slave Trade." Newton's account of the realities of the slave trade was perhaps the most detailed then in circulation. It contributed greatly to the success of the English Abolitionist movement.

Contents

Acknowledgments

Many people have contributed to this project, at various stages, through inspiration, encouragement, thoughtful discussion of my ideas and theories, and careful reading of numerous drafts. I would like to thank all of them, especially Fran Ansley, Susan Appleton, Kate Bartlett, Martha Chamallas, Ruth Colker, Neil Gotanda, Ian Haney López, Margaret Johnson, Dan Keating, Pauline Kim, Richard Lazarus, Helan Page, Robert Post, Peter Wiedenbeck, and Stephanie Wildman. My thanks as well to the students in my constitutional law and critical jurisprudence courses, most particularly members of my Critical Race Theory seminar in 1992. The social science material herein benefited greatly from the very able research assistance of Loretta Haggard.

There are two individuals without whom this book simply would not have been possible. My friend and colleague Kathy Goldwasser helped me in all of the ways mentioned above; her insightful commentary on endless drafts and revisions kept me steadily on course as this project unfolded. Finally, and certainly not least, I could not have completed any part of this work without the tireless encouragement and support, conversation and commentary of my life partner Dayna Deck.

* * *

This book draws from several previously published articles. See Barbara J. Flagg, *"Was Blind, But Now I See": White*

Race Consciousness and the Requirement of Discriminatory Intent, 91 Mich. L. Rev. 953 (1993); Barbara J. Flagg, *Enduring Principle: On Race, Process, and Constitutional Law,* 82 Calif. L. Rev. 935 (1994); Barbara J. Flagg, *Fashioning a Title VII Remedy for Transparently White Subjective Decisionmaking,* 104 Yale L.J. 2009 (1995); Barbara J. Flagg, *Changing the Rules: Some Preliminary Thoughts on Doctrinal Reform, Indeterminacy, and Whiteness,* 11 Berkeley Women's L.J. 250 (1996).

[1]

Introduction

THE MOST STRIKING characteristic of whites' consciousness of whiteness is that most of the time we don't have any. I call this the *transparency phenomenon:* the tendency of whites not to think about whiteness. Instead, white people externalize race. For most whites, most of the time, to think or speak about race is to think or speak about people of color, or perhaps, at times, to reflect on oneself (or other whites) in relation to people of color. But we tend not to think of ourselves or our racial cohort as racially distinctive. Whites' "consciousness" of whiteness is predominantly *unconsciousness* of whiteness. We perceive and interact with other whites as individuals who have no significant racial characteristics. In the same vein, the white person is unlikely to see or describe himself in racial terms, perhaps in part because his white peers do not regard him as racially distinctive. Whiteness is a transparent quality when whites interact with whites in the absence of people of color. Whiteness attains opacity, becomes apparent to the white mind, only in relation to, and in contrast with, the "color" of non-whites.

This is not to say that white people are oblivious to the race of other whites.[1] Race is undeniably a powerful determinant of social status and so is always noticed, in a way that eye color, for example, may not be. However, whites' social dominance allows us to relegate our own racial specificity to the realm of the subconscious. Whiteness is the racial norm. In this culture the black person, not the white, is the one who is different.[2] The black, not the white, is racially distinctive. Once an individual is identified as white, his distinctively racial characteristics need no longer be conceptualized in racial terms; he becomes effectively raceless in the eyes of other whites. Whiteness is always a salient personal characteristic, but once identified, it fades almost instantaneously from white consciousness into transparency.

The best "evidence" for the pervasiveness of the transparency phenomenon will be the white reader's own experience: Critically assessing our habitual ways of thinking about ourselves and about other white people should bring transparency into full view.[3] The questions that follow may provide some direction for the reader's reflections. In what situations do you describe yourself as white? Would you be likely to include "white" on a list of three adjectives that describe you?[4] Do you think about your race as a factor in the way other whites treat you? For example, think about the last time some white clerk or salesperson treated you deferentially, or the last time the first taxi to come along stopped for you. Did you think, "That wouldn't have happened if I weren't white"? Are you conscious of yourself as white when you find yourself in a room occupied only by white people? What if there are people of color present? What if the room is mostly nonwhite?

Do you attribute your successes or failures in life to your whiteness? Do you reflect on the ways your educational and occupational opportunities have been enhanced by your whiteness? What about the life courses of others? In your experience, at the time of Justice Souter's nomination, how much attention did his race receive in conversations among whites about his abilities and prospects for confirmation? Did you or your white acquaintances speculate on the ways his whiteness might have contributed to his success, how his race may have affected his character and personality, or how his whiteness might predispose him to a racially skewed perspective on legal issues?

If your lover or spouse is white, how frequently do you reflect on that fact? Do you think of your white friends as your white friends, other than in contrast with your friends who are not white? Do you try to understand the ways your shared whiteness affects the interactions between yourself and your white partner, friends, and acquaintances? For example, perhaps you have become aware of the absence of people of color on some occasion. Did you move beyond that moment of recognition to consider how the group's uniform whiteness affected its interactions, agenda, process, or decisions? Do you inquire about the ways white persons you know have dealt with the fact, and privilege, of their whiteness?

Imagine that I am describing to you a third individual who is not known to you. I say, for example, "She's good looking, but rather quiet," or "He's tall, dark, and handsome." If I do not specify the race of the person so described, is it not culturally appropriate, and expected, for you to assume she or he is white?[5]

*   *   *

Transparency casts doubt on the concept of race-neutral decisionmaking. The criteria upon which white decisionmakers rely when making a decision may be as vulnerable to the transparency phenomenon as is the race of white people itself. At a minimum, transparency counsels that we not accept seemingly neutral criteria of decision at face value. Most whites live and work in settings that are wholly or predominantly white. Thus whites rely on primarily white referents in formulating the norms and expectations that become the criteria used by white decisionmakers. Given whites' tendency to be unaware of whiteness, it's likely that white decisionmakers mistakenly identify as race-neutral personal characteristics, traits, and behaviors that are in fact closely associated with whiteness. The ways in which transparency might infect white decisionmaking are many and varied. Consider the following story.

A predominantly white Nominating Committee is considering the candidacy of Delores, a black woman, for a seat on the majority white Board of Directors of a national public interest organization. Delores is the sole proprietor of a small business that supplies technical computer services to other businesses. She founded the company eleven years ago; it now grosses over a million dollars annually and employs seven people in addition to the owner. Delores' resume indicates that she dropped out of high school at sixteen. She later obtained a G.E.D. but did not attend college. She was able to open her business in part because of a state program designed to encourage the formation of minority business enterprises.

Delores' resume also reveals many years of participation at the local and state levels in a variety of civic and public interest organizations, including two that focus on issues that are of central concern for the national organization that is now considering her. In fact, she came to the Committee's attention because she is considered a leader on those issues in her state.

During Delores' interview with the Nominating Committee, several white members question her closely about the operation of her business. They seek detailed financial information that she becomes increasingly reluctant to provide. Finally, the questioning turns to her educational background. "Why," one white committee member inquires, "didn't you go to college later, when you were financially able to do so?" "Will you be comfortable on a Board where everyone else has at least a college degree?" another asks. Delores, perhaps somewhat defensively, responds that she is perfectly able to hold her own with college graduates; she deals with them every day in her line of work. In any event, she says, she does not see that her past educational history is as relevant to the position for which she is being considered as is her present ability to analyze the issues confronting the national organization. Why don't they ask her hypothetical policy questions of the sort the Board regularly addresses if they want to see what she can do?

The interview concludes on a tense note. After some delib-
eration, the Committee forwards Delores' name to the full
Board, but with strong reservations. "We found her to be
quite hostile," the Committee reports. "She has a solid history of working on our issue, but she might be a disruptive
presence at Board meetings."

At least three elements of the decisionmaking process in
this story may have been influenced by the transparency
phenomenon. We can examine the first of these only if we
assume that the white committee members would question
every Board candidate who operates a small business in ex-
actly the same manner they queried Delores. (If they have
subjected her to more intense inquiry, perhaps reflecting unconscious skepticism concerning a black woman's ability to
establish and manage a successful, highly technical small
business, the situation ought to be analyzed as an example of
stereotyping rather than transparency).[6] Assuming no such
racial (or, for that matter, gender) stereotyping was at work,
so that the questioning was in fact uniform for black and
white candidates, it still does not follow that those candidates
would interpret the inquiries in the same way. It's predictable
that a black interviewee might take exception to such a line
of questioning because of the common white image of blacks
as not very intelligent; given that the candidate has no prior
knowledge of her white interviewers, she might reasonably
wonder whether the questions arise from that image, even if
they in fact do not. A white candidate, on the other hand,
would come to the interview without any history of being
viewed in that way, and so should be expected to respond to
the line of questioning with greater equanimity. Transpar-

ency—here, the unconscious assumption that all interviewees will, or should, respond to a given line of questioning the way a white candidate (or the interviewers themselves) would respond—may account for the white questioners' inability to anticipate the more subtle implications their queries might have for the nonwhite interviewee.

Second, the white committee members may be imposing white educational norms as well. Anyone smart enough to attend college surely would do so, they might assume. However, whites attend college at a higher rate than blacks. The committee members' assumption takes into account neither the realities of the inner city schools this woman attended, nor the personal and cultural influences that caused her to decide to drop out of high school, nor the ways the cost-benefit analysis of a college education might appear different to a black person than to a white person. Delores' business success suggests that she made a rational and effective decision to develop her business rather than divide her energies between the business and school. Transparency may blind the white committee members to the whiteness of the educational norms they and their organization appear to take for granted.

The most troubling and perhaps least obviously race-specific aspect of the story is the ultimate assessment of Delores as "hostile." This seemingly neutral adjective is in fact race-specific in this context insofar as it rests on norms and expectations that are themselves race-specific. To characterize this candidate's responses as hostile is to judge them inappropriate. Such a judgment presupposes an unstated norm of appropriate behavior in that setting, one that reflects white experience, priorities, and life strategies. The committee members' expectations did not take into account some of the realities of black life in the United States that form part of the context in which the black candidate operates. The transparency of white experience and the norms that flow from it permitted the Nominating Committee to transmute the appropriate responses of a black candidate into a seemingly neutral assessment of "hostility."

* * *

Transparently white decisionmaking is one form of institutional racism, defined as any institutional practice that systematically creates or perpetuates racial advantage or disadvantage. This conception of racism differs from ones that revolve around notions of individual prejudice and hostility, and in fact carries no requirement that the individuals who created the institution in question or who participate in it harbor any conscious dislike of, or animus toward, nonwhites. It is the thesis of this book that even seemingly "benign" participation in racially unjust institutions fully implicates individuals in the maintenance of white supremacy. Those who wish to claim a nonracist white identity must find active ways of dismantling existing systems of racial privilege.

One available strategy is to challenge insistently every example of transparency in white decisionmaking. We can work to reveal the unacknowledged whiteness of facially neutral criteria of decision, and we can adopt strategies that counteract the influence of unrecognized white norms. These approaches permit white decisionmakers to incorporate pluralist[7] means of achieving our otherwise nonracist aims, and thus to contribute to the racial redistribution of social power.

Law might assist in this endeavor, but at present race discrimination law is unresponsive to the transparency phenomenon. Existing laws embody too narrow a concept of race discrimination to include nonobvious forms of institutional racism.[8] Consequently, race discrimination law does not currently provide any legal remedies for discrimination that takes the form of transparently white decisionmaking. In effect, today's race discrimination law is itself a form of institutional racism: By failing to address transparency, it contributes to the maintenance of a racially unjust status quo.

This book explores the contribution a transformed race discrimination law might make to rectifying the effects of the transparency phenomenon. I proceed on the premise that recognizing, analyzing, and devising responses to transparently white decisionmaking in everyday settings and in law is a synergistic enterprise. Our understanding of the ways transparency plays itself out in life can inform our critique of antidiscrimination law, and, conversely, the project of assessing the theoretical foundation, symbolic import, and practical effects of antidiscrimination law can serve as a context in which to reexamine who we, as white people, are and want to be. Accordingly, this book critically analyzes two central examples of race discrimination law with the ultimate objective of exploring the implications of transparency-conscious doctrinal reform, reciprocally, for law and for white race consciousness itself.

The antidiscrimination provisions under examination here

are the Equal Protection Clause of the United States Constitution, which requires government to extend "the equal protection of the laws" without regard to race, and Title VII of the Civil Rights Act of 1964, which proscribes race discrimination in employment. The specific focus of the analysis will be the Equal Protection and Title VII rules governing the use of seemingly neutral criteria of decision that, even when applied evenhandedly, have racially skewed effects; these rules are singled out because transparency is a phenomenon that manifests itself in facially neutral forms. In Equal Protection jurisprudence there is a requirement of discriminatory intent: a judicially created rule that government bears a burden of justification with regard to a practice carrying racially disparate effects only when it can be shown that the practice was adopted with discriminatory intent. As is perhaps obvious, the requirement of discriminatory intent operates as an absolute barrier to recognition of unconscious discrimination, and so fails to provide any foothold for attacking the transparency phenomenon. One might wonder, then, whether jettisoning the intent requirement would produce more satisfactory results. Title VII provides an example of that approach, as it places a requirement of justification upon an employer solely upon proof of disparate effects. However, careful examination reveals that Title VII too falls short with respect to transparently white decisionmaking.

Chapter 2 provides a foundation for the analysis of existing Equal Protection and Title VII rules, and for the formulation of more satisfactory legal doctrines, by sketching the general contours of the universe of racism's various manifestations and locating transparently white decisionmaking on that conceptual map. It then surveys possible antiracist strategies, again with particular emphasis on antiracist responses to transparently white decisionmaking. This chapter explains how transparently white decisionmaking might be countered by adopting a thoroughgoing skepticism regarding the neutrality of seemingly race-neutral decision criteria. Such skepticism amounts to a presumption *against* the race neutrality of apparently neutral criteria of decision, and thus provides an opening for the formulation of criteria more capable of effecting distributive racial justice. The skeptical stance provides a benchmark for the critique of antidiscrimination law.

Chapter 3 scrutinizes the constitutional requirement of discriminatory intent and concludes that it does not provide any point of contact for grappling with the transparency phenomenon in decisionmaking. It then proposes an alternative approach to disparate effects cases that would incorporate the thoroughgoing skepticism just described: Race discrimination law ought to incorporate a presumption that ostensibly race-neutral criteria of decision are in fact race-specific, and thus ought to provide a legal remedy for transparently white decisionmaking, in the absence of a persuasive justification for the challenged practice.

Clearly, the concepts of transparently white decisionmaking, institutional racism, and deliberate skepticism that inform this analysis are not universally shared in American culture. Constitutional interpretation always is a complicated subject, and it is especially so with respect to contested social values. Many legal commentators hold that it is improper for judges to superimpose their own vision of desirable social policy on the constitutional text; accordingly, in their view, constitutional interpretation is performed best when it is an exercise in judicial restraint. This contention is the subject of chapter 4.

Chapter 5 explores the legal regime of Title VII, in which seemingly neutral criteria of decision that produce racially disparate effects are subject to justification even without proof of discriminatory intent, and concludes that even under this approach there are substantial barriers to recognition of, and legal redress for, transparently white decisionmaking. This chapter sets forth two alternative proposals, either of which promises to be more effective in combatting transparency than the current rules. These proposals in turn give rise to another set of concerns: Even if it is desirable for individuals to acknowledge transparency by adopting a skeptical stance regarding their own decisionmaking (and for government voluntarily to do the same), it may be inappropriate for government to require individual employers to do so. These concerns will be addressed in the course of chapter 6's discussion of the foundation and scope of Title VII.

The book concludes with a discussion, in chapter 7, of several jurisprudential and larger implications of the transparency-conscious proposals set forth in chapters 3 through 6. First, I describe the ways in which these modified doctrines reflect a discourse of responsibility rather than a discourse of blame; I argue that the former approach is more productive of the goal of racial remediation than the current one, which carries connotations of criminality and often promotes no more than white guilt and paralysis (and, at times, anger).

Second, I address the problem of legal indeterminacy—that is, the thesis that doctrine alone does not decide legal outcomes. If legal doctrine does not genuinely constrain legal decisionmakers, the reforms proposed here cannot have any practical effect, and thus the project of doctrinal reform is an empty one. I respond to legal indeterminacy by conceiving doctrine as a sort of promise. A promisor binds herself to behave differently than would have been the case had she not promised, even with respect to gratuitous and vague promises. At a minimum, legal doctrine can be analogized to vague promises, and perhaps to gratuitous promises as well, and so constrains in the same way that any such promises constrain. Because promises constrain, different promises constrain differently, and so there is value in promising more rather than less.

Third, I describe how evaluating and enlarging the promises made by whites to nonwhites in the form of antidiscrimination law can benefit the larger project of reconstructing an antiracist white identity.[9] Transparency-conscious race discrimination laws would be one way of employing white privilege—here, the privilege of controlling the formulation of legal doctrine—to the advantage of nonwhites. The key to making this strategy a meaningful one is for whites to make and keep promises that genuinely foster distributive racial justice.

* * *

Every project such as this has its own point of departure; I would like to acknowledge expressly some premises upon which this work proceeds. First, though discussions of race discrimination often begin with, or move quickly to, questions about discrimination against white people, that is not of concern here, because the present topic is the struggle against white supremacy.[10] Several additional points merit more extended discussion: This project assumes that it is appropriate for law to foster racial redistribution, it assumes that subtle forms of institutional racism are worthy of focused attention, and it assumes that doctrinal reform is an enterprise in which everyone can participate.

Some legal theorists contend that redistribution never is an appropriate objective for the law to pursue; that law at most ought to intervene in society to secure the preconditions of autonomous action, such as personal security, and/or to correct "market failures."[11] Some of these theorists might identify the existing racial maldistribution of social power and material goods as evidence of a "market failure," but others would not. In either case, disapproval of redistribution through law is a political position, one which this project does not share. It is the premise of this book—and perhaps an appropriate subject for debate elsewhere—that racial inequality is too pressing a problem to allow any possible tool of remediation, including the law, to be discounted or set aside. More specific contentions that the particular antidiscrimination measures under consideration here—the Equal Protection Clause and Title VII—are not intended to have a redistributive focus will be addressed as each is presented in turn.

Second, this project may be criticized as elitist in its emphasis on subtle forms of institutional racism: What about real-world problems such as poverty and disease, and garden-variety racial hostility? Though I acknowledge that the problems addressed here constitute but one small portion of the ways racism manifests itself, they are not unimportant. It seems fair to say that the transparency phenomenon, because it concerns discretionary decisionmaking, has its greatest impact on the lives of relatively well-positioned nonwhites. It is just this characteristic that makes it significant, however. A reduction in the quantum of transparently white decisionmaking would result in more nonwhites gaining positions of authority without having to assimilate to white norms. One can hope that such a redistribution of decisionmaking power would in the long run benefit the less well-positioned nonwhite as well.

Finally, I emphasize that this project, fostering an antiracist white identity by adopting legal doctrines that promise racial redistribution, is one in which there is a role for everyone. Certainly, all participants in the legal system have a part to play in law's evolution, and each of them who is white is as well-positioned to take responsibility for white supremacy as any other white person. However, it should be emphasized that there are ways individuals who do not participate formally in the legal system also can contribute to the transformation of race discrimination law.

It is not difficult to envision the role judges can play in doctrinal reform. Because constitutional law has its source in relatively opened-ended constitutional texts (such as "the equal protection of the laws"), its practical content is largely a matter of judicial interpretation. Even statutes, which have their source either in a legislature or directly in the popular will (in the case of laws enacted by initiative or referendum), are subject to interpretation by judges when they apply statutes to particular cases. To the extent a given constitutional text or statute permits, then, doctrinal reform is well within the power of judges to accomplish. Indeed, one finds clear examples of this power in the areas of law examined here: Both the requirement of discriminatory intent in constitutional law and the rules for establishing disparate impact under Title VII are judicially created. Thus judges could, if persuaded by the arguments here, institute those reforms in a straightforward manner.

It is equally clear that legislators have the power to effect doctrinal reform, certainly with respect to statutes (subject to constitutional limitations and, in some jurisdictions, review by referendum), and the power to propose constitutional reform by way of constitutional amendment. Moreover, Section 5 of the Fourteenth Amendment grants Congress the authority to "enforce, by appropriate legislation, the provisions of this article," which sometimes has been interpreted as granting Congress the power to expand the scope of its protections.[12] Thus Congress certainly could clarify the rules governing Title VII disparate impact cases in a transparency-conscious manner, and perhaps could find ways, under Section 5, to exert pressure on the constitutional requirement of discriminatory intent.

Litigants and their attorneys also play important roles in the process of doctrinal reform, by bringing cases that present courts with the opportunity to adopt more transparency-conscious doctrines, and by providing those courts with legal analyses that would facilitate the desired doctrinal results. The foundation of today's constitutional race discrimination law—this century's Equal Protection cases up to and including *Brown v. Board of Education*—as well as most of today's constitutional sex discrimination doctrine, for example, are the products of concerted and sustained litigation efforts that were markedly successful in changing the law.[13]

Finally, law professors too have a part to play in the process of doctrinal reform, in their capacities as both scholars and teachers. As scholars, we can propose doctrinal reforms in the hope that judges and other legal actors will take them to heart, and we sometimes provide the theoretical foundation that facilitates such change. As teachers, we can present lawyers-to-be with a vision of doctrine that is not limited to the way things are today, and encourage them to take on an active role in the process of doctrinal transformation. Conversely, students can request and expect institutions of legal education to provide training in the process of legal change, alongside training in the legal status quo.

Undoubtedly, those whose lives enmesh them in the legal system—whether as parties, judges, legislators, attorneys, professors, or students—are more likely to come in contact with the possibility of working for doctrinal reform than those whose lives are less intimately connected with the law. We should not conclude, however, that the project of reforming race discrimination law is one in which the latter cannot participate. First, in this society law ostensibly reflects the will of the people. Everyone can join in working for legislative change, in the usual political manner. Were there a white consensus on the need for transparency-conscious legislation, it likely would appear in relatively short order. More subtly, law is an embodiment of society's norms, and so a transformed white race consciousness would make its way into judicially created legal doctrines as well, though perhaps in a less immediate manner.

Moreover, there is a dual objective to be served by the

examination of race discrimination law undertaken here: to transform white race consciousness as well as to transform the law. Developing an antiracist white identity is to be valued for its own sake, whether or not it finds expression in reformed legal doctrines. A transformed white race consciousness is instrumentally valuable because of its potential impact on all forms of individual and institutional racism. Additionally, constructing an antiracist white identity is intrinsically valuable because it is morally the right thing to do.

The two objectives—doctrinal reform and transforming white race consciousness—reinforce one another. The more conscious whites become of the myriad forms of white privilege, the better positioned we are to renounce it, including renunciation that takes the form of redistributive legal doctrines. Conversely, understanding existing law and the distance between it and a racially just legal regime contributes to an enhanced understanding of white privilege. Indeed, the two objectives are mutually interdependent: In the end it is impossible to imagine a genuinely racially redistributive legal regime in the absence of a developed antiracist white racial identity, and it is equally impossible to envision an authentically antiracist white identity that does not give up concrete forms of social and material power.

[2]

An Overview of Race and Racism

T HOUGH THE TRANSPARENCY phenomenon itself should be easily recognizable to whites in this society, the proposition that it is a form of racism may not be equally uncontroversial. This chapter provides a framework for understanding the role of transparency as a tool of white supremacy. First, I explore the concept of race as a social process, rather than biological "fact." Second, I locate the transparency phenomenon on a conceptual map of racism, with the objective of examining useful strategies for combatting racism in its various forms and manifestations. In particular, the technique of skepticism that emerges as an appropriate and effective device for addressing transparency provides a benchmark for the evaluation and reform of race discrimination law.

What Is Race?

For most people, I suspect, and almost certainly for most whites, race carries a pervasive biological connotation, much like an individual's sex. One's race is thought to be a matter of inheritance or descent, and thus outside the individual's and society's control. Of course, we do recognize that race has social implications; for example, many white liberals hold that race should not matter in the distribution of social goods, as it does in today's society. That is effectively an acknowledgment that race has a social component; it clearly might have a social meaning different from its present one. Nevertheless, this social aspect of race is considered secondary and contingent, while its biological roots are regarded as primary and immutable.

However, it can be argued that this conventional understanding of race is inverted: Race is primarily a social phenomenon, and only secondarily a biological "fact." Three lines of argument converge to support this conclusion. First, there no longer are (if there ever were) clear lines of descent to ground a biological conception of race. Second, racial categories exhibit extreme variability across cultures. Third, racial categories shift rapidly within cultures. Consider each of these contentions in turn.

Much scientific evidence now indicates that there is no such thing as "racial purity." Everyone carries an admixture of genetic material traceable to several "racial groups": no one can claim an unequivocal racial identity.[1] Genetic research shows that variations within "racial groups" often exceed variations between such groups. Thus the individual cannot meaningfully be ascribed a single biological racial identity; she has genetic links with other groups as strong as or stronger than the links with the group with which she is conventionally identified.

Given that race cannot be linked to genetic composition, the theorist who wishes to defend the proposition that race is fundamentally biological might turn to appearance as the definitive racial characteristic. But this approach founders on the recognition that an individual is often assigned a racial identity inconsistent with his or her appearance. Homer Plessy, for example, was denied a seat (in 1892) in a "white" railroad car in spite of his "white" appearance because the railway conductor "knew" him to be "black."[2]

Racial categories may be more fluid than conventional wisdom realizes. Systems of racial classification vary across cultures. Some other cultures recognize different and more numerous racial categories than does ours. In Brazil, for example, one researcher identified forty distinct racial classifications.[3] Moreover, membership in a particular category is not always immutable. Again, Brazil provides an example: "Brazilians say 'Money whitens,' meaning that the richer a dark man gets the lighter will be the category to which he will be assigned by his friends, relatives and business associates."[4]

Racial categories also vary within a given culture over time. In the United States, the system of racial classification has changed more often and more rapidly than many realize. In the 1800s, Latin Americans often were described both by nationality and by race. For example, a Mexican might be white, Indian, black, or Asian.[5] Thus there was no analogue to today's "racial" category "Hispanic." Another example is to be found in the perception, during roughly the same period, that Chinese immigrants were racially similar to blacks; today's racial imagery sees those groups as quite distinct.[6]

Race, then, is a plastic, sociopolitical phenomenon; its meaning responds to changes in time, place, and circumstance.[7] What does it mean for the study of racism to give up the concept that racial identity is an immutable biological fact? Some might argue that recognizing the social construction of race lends additional force to the argument for colorblindness as social and legal policy: Because race turns out not to be "real" (i.e., biological), it ought not to be afforded legal or social significance. However, colorblindness progressively reveals itself to be an inadequate social policy if the ultimate goal is substantive racial justice. Blacks continue to inhabit a very different America than do whites. They experience higher rates of poverty and unemployment[8] and are more likely to live in environmentally undesirable locations than whites.[9] They have more frequent and more severe medical problems, higher mortality rates, and receive less comprehensive health care than whites.[10] Blacks continue disproportionately to attend inferior and inadequate primary and secondary schools.[11] Proportionately fewer blacks than whites complete college, and those who do so still confront the "glass ceiling" after graduation.[12] Blacks are no better off by many of these measures than they were twenty years ago,[13] and in the recent past even the colorblindness principle itself, once seen as a promise of a brighter future for blacks, has been deployed instead to block further black economic progress.[14]

Recognizing the social construction of race, I believe, impels one in quite a different direction from the dead-end policy of colorblindness. It means that individuals, especially privileged individuals, and groups, especially privileged groups, have more of an opportunity to take responsibility for the meaning of racial identity than might otherwise appear to be the case. The fact that race is not inevitable calls for special consideration of the significance afforded it in a given culture.

In this society, race is an element of social stratification. That is, one's social status depends in part on one's racial identity. Moreover, race is independent of other stratifying characteristics, such as sex, wealth, age, religion, sexual orientation, physical disability, education, or national origin, though its specific impact varies with these other factors. Thus the social meaning of being white is different if one is female or male, old or young, straight or gay, and so on, and the same is true for every other racial category. However, the absence of any single essence of whiteness (or any other racial classification) does not mean that race is reducible to any other characteristic. Race plays an independent, though complex, role in the process of social stratification.

That race is socially constructed thus impels reexamination of whiteness itself. It is indisputable that in the United States whites occupy the uppermost position on the racial dimension of social stratification, a reality that together with the plasticity of race leads us to ask whether whites can or should be comfortable with a racial identity composed almost entirely of social privilege. Assuming that the answer to that question is negative, seeing race as socially constructed provides a framework in which to recast whiteness as the dismantling of privilege, rather than its realization.

Law plays a role in the social construction of race. Some laws have a direct and obvious impact, such as laws incorporating racial classifications. Until 1952, for example, whiteness was a prerequisite for becoming a naturalized citizen of the United States.[15] Ian Haney López has described a series of cases in which courts were called upon to construe this racial requirement; in these cases "common knowledge" gradually superseded "scientific" knowledge as the standard by which an individual's racial identity was to be established.[16] Thus the statutory racial prerequisite both reflected and reinforced socially constructed racial categories.

It is worth noting that legal definitions of racial categories are not entirely a thing of the past. In 1970 Louisiana passed a law that in effect defined as "white" a person having one thirty-second or less of "Negro blood." [17] Though that law was repealed in 1983, it was relied upon in a 1987 case in which several siblings sought to compel the state Department of Health and Human Resources to change their birth certificates, which designated their parents as "colored." One of the plaintiffs, Susie Guillory Phipps, who regarded herself as white, testified that she was "sick for three days" upon learning that her birth certificate classified both of her parents as colored.[18] Just as a government act—the racial identification of her parents on her birth certificate—had created her "problem," she sought a remedy through a legal reclassification of her parents' race.

Law also shapes the social meaning of race through its impact on social interaction, which in turn affects morphology itself. Miscegenation laws and Jim Crow segregation laws, for instance, enforced racial separation in ways that affected individuals' social experience. One can only conclude that these laws had some effect; interracial marriage almost certainly would have been more common had such laws never been enacted. Moreover, reduced contact between races must serve to enhance the ideology of racial difference.

Antidiscrimination laws bear a somewhat different connection to the social meaning of race than do racial classification laws or laws regulating the terms of social interaction. First, antidiscrimination laws reflect whites' conception of race and racism. Though existing race discrimination laws tend to embody limited conceptions of "race discrimination," a broader understanding of discrimination may be gained by examining the processes by which race is socially constructed, and that more comprehensive vision might find meaningful expression in revised antidiscrimination doctrines. Second, antidiscrimination law can play a significant role in the social construction of whiteness. Because law is coercive, it can effect redistribution of social goods, and thus can serve as a vehicle for the dismantling of white privilege. Accordingly, suitably reformed doctrines might aid the social reconstruction of white identity in an antiracist direction.[19]

What Is Racism?

"Racism" is used in a number of related ways, which generally revolve around the notion of a disapproved recognition of race. We say that someone is racist when he or she has afforded race a significance we think it ought not to have, either with respect to characterization or consequence. That is, it can be considered "racist" to think or say that black people are inferior to whites, that Asians are inscrutable, or that Native Americans are lazy. However, maintaining an institution that systematically disadvantages blacks also can be characterized as racist. It has in common with the earlier examples the feature that race matters, in a way that is disapproved by the person employing the label "racist." The varieties of racism call for closer examination.

The most common usages of the term "racism" implicate individual, psychological concepts. For example, hostility toward, or dislike of, persons of another race is perhaps the most widely recognized conception of racism. Along the same lines, persons who regard individuals of another race as inferior beings, or who believe that their own culture is superior to that of other races, often are characterized as "racist."

Such racial attitudes may be conscious or unconscious. Some social scientists acknowledge these two possibilities by differentiating between prejudice and stereotyping.[20] Prejudice consists of conscious beliefs, propositions that an individual knowingly accepts as true. Stereotypes, on the other hand, consist of attitudes acquired early in life and, in this use of the term, generally function outside one's conscious control. For instance, some persons who grew up in the South report feeling "squeamish" upon touching the hand of a black person, even though they harbor no conscious ill will toward blacks.[21]

Of course, this definition of "stereotype" departs in some respects from common usage, which recognizes as well the existence of conscious generalizations about racial groups, and sometimes labels such beliefs "stereotypes." Moreover, some such conscious beliefs appear not to be negative, as when a white person consciously entertains the view that "blacks are better athletes." However, further analysis reveals that such beliefs almost always incorporate a negative subtext, such as "blacks are better athletes, but they aren't as smart."[22] Thus a white person's conscious, superficially positive stereotype of nonwhites most likely reflects an unconscious negative image, and so will be included under the heading of unconscious negative personal attitudes.

Social scientists describe as "high prejudiced" persons whose conscious personal beliefs are congruent with negative cultural stereotypes of blacks and other members of racial minority groups.[23] "Low prejudiced" persons are those whose conscious personal beliefs diverge from the negative stereotypes that they too carry.[24] These terms suggest that unconscious negative attitudes toward persons of other races exist relatively independently of conscious racial beliefs. That feature of individual racism has implications for the ways racism may be combatted and controlled, as will be described below.

"Racist" also may be used to characterize an institution that systematically creates or perpetuates racial advantage and disadvantage. Institutional racism (defined by the racially skewed effects of institutional practices) functions under the wing of a variety of ideological devices. In some cases, more common in the past than today, social institutions are the overt expression of racial hostility, or of widely shared beliefs in racial and/or cultural inferiority. Jim Crow social arrangements provide an example; they rested on an undisguised "racist" ideology. However, institutional racism also may be supported by an egalitarian ideology that operates in defense of racial advantage, but superficially endorses racial equality.[25] For example, a job requirement of a high school education, adopted in an era and a location in which almost no blacks attained a high school diploma, would function to disadvantage blacks while appearing to rest on a nonracial conception of job qualifications.

Individual participants in racist social institutions may be located at any point on the continuum of individual racism. In the case of an institution that is superficially egalitarian, individual participation might be the consequence of disguised or undisguised hostility or prejudice, but it might equally be the product of inattention, indifference, or ignorance. Some "low prejudiced" persons might even find comfort in an "egalitarian" institutional setting that perpetuates racial advantage precisely because the outcomes conform to unexamined racial stereotypes, while the prevailing ideology coincides with the individual's own nonprejudiced beliefs.

Numerous superficially egalitarian institutional practices result in racial injustice. These include, for example, processes of marginalization and tokenism that permit an institution to appear inclusive, but effectively distance nonwhites from positions of power, authority, and security.[26] A second category of seemingly benign institutional practices encompasses ostensibly race-neutral decisionmaking. The high school diploma requirement cited above provides an example, as do high union initiation fees (because of blacks' relatively weaker economic situation) and the practice of advertising job openings only in major newspapers (because these papers often are not as easily accessible in "black" parts of town, and so are not equally available to black job seekers as to whites).[27] Each of these examples illustrates a decisionmaking criterion that disadvantages nonwhites because of the effects of other social institutions and realities. Another form of institutional racism involves multiple criteria of decision that permit a decisionmaker to select at will one of several bases for a particular decision. In the employment setting, for example, leadership potential, education, and experience within the organization might constitute coequal grounds for promotion. These parallel criteria provide an avenue for the operation of unconscious racial bias, hostility, or stereotyping, because they can offer a plausible foundation for each of several outcomes. This sort of decisionmaking represents an instance of institutional racism if it actually results in disadvantaging nonwhites; it is institutional because it is the institution that makes the choice to implement a regime of multiple, potentially shifting decision criteria.

The transparency phenomenon plays yet a third role in the formation of egalitarian institutional racism, insofar as it fosters whites decisionmakers' tendency to adopt and apply transparently white criteria of decision. These criteria systematically favor whites, and thus institutions that rely on such ostensibly race-neutral criteria afford substantial advantages to whites over nonwhites even when decisionmakers intend to effect substantive racial justice.

Among the various forms racism may take, this book is primarily concerned with the latter form of ideologically egalitarian institutional racism, and specifically with antidiscrimination law's response to it. I place a special emphasis on the role transparently white decisionmaking plays in structuring and maintaining seemingly egalitarian racist institutions, and I explore legal doctrines that might be more productive antiracist tools than those in effect at present. Before turning to the legal realm, however, it might be useful to examine nonlegal methods of combatting racism.

Combatting Racism

Return to the hypothetical case of Delores, introduced at the beginning of chapter 1. Under consideration for a seat on the Board of Directors of a national public interest organization, she is about to be interviewed by a Nominating Committee, a subdivision of the Board of Directors, both of which are predominantly white. Suppose that there is a representative individual who harbors each of the forms of individual racism on the Nominating Committee.

The individual who is a conscious and overt racist will, of course, simply argue that there is no place on the Board of Directors for blacks, either because they are unpleasant to be around, they are incapable of performing the tasks required of a Board member, or because they "have values different from ours." These views, however, are disapproved in substantial segments of today's society, and so a person who endorses one or more of those propositions more likely would not express them, but would consciously seek other ways to subvert Delores' candidacy. Such an individual would be a covert individual racist.

By definition, conscious racists have no reason to combat

racism; they approve it. However, the national organization might choose to adopt antiracist policies. With respect to overtly racist Board members, both identification and remedy are relatively straightforward. The national organization might express its antiracist position by immediately removing from the Board any member who expresses overtly prejudiced sentiments.

The problem of formulating an antiracist policy is somewhat more complicated in the case of the covert individual racist, because the task of identification is more difficult. A pattern of voting against minority candidates would be one significant indicator of the presence of covert racism. Thus the organization might adopt some procedure for evaluating the continued presence on the Board of an individual who exhibited such a voting pattern. A procedure to ferret out the covert but conscious racist would be designed to differentiate between a pattern of negative votes motivated by race, and a similar pattern actually motivated by nonracial concerns.

The final variety of individual racism represented on this Nominating Committee is the "low prejudiced" person, who endorses no racist personal beliefs but who at times acts on unconscious racial stereotypes. During Delores' interview, this person questions her closely about the operation of her business. The committee member seeks unusually detailed financial information, in a manner that suggests skepticism concerning this black woman's ability to establish and manage a successful, highly technical small business.

Social scientists who defend the distinction between prejudice and stereotyping explain that even an individual who holds no prejudiced beliefs may act on the basis of ingrained and habitual attitudes, such as the stereotypical judgment that blacks are incompetent. If the stereotype has a longer history and is more frequently reinforced (for example, in media images of blacks) than the incongruent personal belief that blacks are as capable as whites, the stereotype will prevail in determining the individual's response to a black subject.

In chapter 1 I set aside the possibility that this close questioning was an expression of unconscious stereotyping, instead analyzing it as an example of applying a transparently white norm regarding appropriate topics and styles of information-gathering. In reality, whether a particular episode ought to be characterized as a case of stereotyping or of transparency depends on whether the actor treats blacks and whites similarly or differently. Stereotyping involves the application of unconscious attitudes *about blacks*; it will engender different treatment of blacks and whites, because whites will not be viewed through the same lens as blacks. In contrast, transparently white decisionmaking consists of the *uniform application* of a norm or expectation that is in fact white-specific; it too disadvantages nonwhites, but it does so in spite of even-handed treatment.

Thus, the questioning Delores underwent regarding her financial situation ought to be seen as an example of stereotyping if the questioner would have behaved differently if he or she had been interviewing a white candidate. The same behavior should be analyzed as an instance of transparently white decisionmaking if the interviewer in fact would have proceeded in the same manner even had the candidate been white.

The strategy for combatting stereotyping follows from the analysis set forth above: The individual should seek ways to inhibit the stereotypical response and to activate a response based on his nonprejudiced beliefs, which would result in his treating black and white persons in the same way. The basic ingredients of this strategy are the recognition of race and the conscious reevaluation of learned stereotypes. That is, the unconscious discriminator may combat stereotypical thinking by reminding himself that he is interviewing a *black* candidate, and then by asking himself what stereotypes or generalizations that fact carries for him. The organization itself might prompt the same reflections, say by including similar points in a handbook containing guidelines for interviewing Board candidates.

*   *   *

In general, strategies for combatting institutional racism mirror strategies for combatting individual racism. Institutions that reproduce racial hierarchy and are supported by overtly racist ideology are analogous to conscious individual racism, and ideologically egalitarian racist institutions are analogous to the "low prejudiced" unconscious racist. With respect to ideologically racist institutions, the only feasible course is sanction and control; no internal antiracist impetus operates.

Just as with the individual unconscious discriminator, consciousness-raising is the strongest antiracist strategy with regard to ideologically egalitarian institutional racism. Sound antiracist strategies include consciousness of race, consciousness of race-specific outcomes, that is, of the racial distribution of goods produced or distributed by the institution in question, and consciousness of the processes that produce inequitable racial outcomes. In addition, of course, one must be willing to alter the offending processes in order to, and in ways that really do, produce racially just results. The systemic nature of institutional racism often demands a collective response.

However, transparently white decision criteria pose a special difficulty. One may be tempted to conclude that what is needed is a more reliable technique for distinguishing genuinely race-neutral criteria of decision from those that only appear neutral. The analyses in chapter 1 of the Nominating Committee members' failure to recognize white-specific norms might demonstrate only that they—and we—can do better. Perhaps we could use this and similar stories as points of departure for an attempt to correct white misperceptions of white-specific criteria of decision.

Three considerations, however, counsel against attempting to formulate a "rule" that would distinguish transparent from authentically race-neutral decision criteria. First, Delores' story presents only rudimentary examples of transparently white norms. Doubtless more complex and subtle stories of transparency might be told, for which the task of recognition and analysis would be significantly more difficult. At the same time, white decisionmakers make the relatively simple errors illustrated by this story quite frequently, and some whites will resist or reject (or both) even the analyses I have proffered. Whites as a group lack the experience necessary even to begin to construct the analytic tools that would ground a comprehensive theory of transparency.

Second, transparency probably attaches more to word usages than to the words themselves. For example, "hostility" may not have a race-laden connotation in every instance in which a white decisionmaker employs it. The context of use—the combination of speaker, audience, decisionmaking process, and purpose—more likely supplies the racial content of the term "hostile" as applied. Thus, a general analysis of transparency might have to be, paradoxically, situation specific, thereby exponentially increasing the complexity of the theoretical task.

Finally, the assumption that we can get better at identifying genuinely race-neutral decisionmaking presupposes that such a thing is possible. However, placing any confidence in the concept of race neutrality is premature at best, because little supports it other than whites' subjective experience, itself subject to the transparency phenomenon. The available empirical evidence points in the opposite direction. Social scientists' work shows that race nearly always influences the outcomes of discretionary decisionmaking processes, including those in which the decisionmaker relies on criteria thought to be race-neutral. There is, of course, no conclusive evidence that no instances of genuine race neutrality exist, but neither is there conclusive evidence to the contrary. The pervasiveness of the transparency phenomenon militates against an unsupported faith by whites in the reality of race-neutral decisionmaking.

I recommend instead that whites adopt a deliberate and thoroughgoing skepticism regarding the race neutrality of ostensibly neutral criteria of decision. This stance has the potential to improve the distribution across races of goods and power currently controlled by whites. In addition, skepticism may help to foster the development of an antiracist white racial identity that does not posit whites as superior to blacks.

Operating from a presumption that seemingly neutral decision criteria are in fact white-specific may prompt white decisionmakers to engage in the sort of analysis presented earlier, when they would not otherwise have done so. Heightened awareness of formerly overlooked race specificity may, in turn, lead to formulation of modified criteria of decision that are more attuned to, and more productive of, distributive racial justice. Had the white Nominating Committee members been aware of the race-specific dimensions of their questions concerning Delores' business enterprise and educational background, they most likely would not have asked those questions. Perhaps they would have gone so far as to adopt the course suggested by Delores herself—to pose for her hypothetical policy issues, her responses to which likely would have been more revealing of the contributions she would make as a black Board member.

Even when he looks for it, however, the white decisionmaker may not always be able to uncover the hidden racial content of the criteria he employs. In those instances, the skeptical stance may function to promote distributive justice in two different ways. First, the skeptical decisionmaker may opt to temper his judgment with a simultaneous acknowledgment of his uncertainty concerning nonobvious racial specificity. Thus, in the Nominating Committee example, the decisionmakers would have forwarded the nomination with a recommendation something like the following: "We experienced this candidate as somewhat hostile, but we are not sure whether there is some racial element that we do not fully understand influencing our judgment." The impact of whiteness on the final decision may thus be mitigated even in the absence of a complete analysis of transparency. Delores is more likely to be accepted by the full Board on a recommendation that does not unequivocally describe her as "hostile." Even assuming she winds up seated on the Board in either scenario, she certainly would be in a better position to have her views heard and fairly considered if she arrived without the unqualified label of hostility attached to her in advance.

Second, white decisionmakers might choose to develop pluralistic criteria of decision as a prophylactic against covert white specificity. In this approach the Committee would allow a nominee to characterize the qualifications, perspective, and experience she would bring to the Board if selected, with whatever emphasis she might choose to place on the fact that she would be a nonwhite member of a predominantly white group. The Committee would then report the candidate's assessment of her qualifications to the full Board and allow that policymaking body to decide whether the organization's ultimate goals might be furthered by the addition of this candidate. This strategy seeks to minimize the effect of transparently race-specific decision criteria by substituting, whenever possible, criteria formulated by the nonwhite candidate.

The skeptical stance may contribute to the development of an antiracist white racial identity by relativizing white norms. Even whites who do not harbor any conscious or unconscious belief in the superiority of white people participate in the maintenance of white supremacy whenever we impose white norms without acknowledging their whiteness. Any serious effort to dismantle white supremacy must include measures to dilute the effect of whites' dominant status, which carries with it the power to define as well as to decide. Because the skeptical stance prevents the unthinking imposition of white norms, it encourages white decisionmakers to consider adopting nonwhite ways of doing business, so that the formerly unquestioned white-specific criterion of decision becomes just one option among many. The skeptical stance thus can be instrumental in the development of a relativized white race consciousness, in which the white decisionmaker is conscious of the whiteness and contingency of white norms.

Most white people have no experience of a genuine cultural pluralism, one in which whites' perspectives, behavioral expectations, and values are not taken to be the standard from which all other cultural norms deviate. Whites therefore have no experiential basis for assessing the benefits of participating in a pluralist society so defined. Assuming that prevailing egalitarian mores preclude white supremacy as a justification for the maintenance of the status quo, adopting the skeptical stance in the interest of exploring cultural pluralism seems the most appropriate course of action for any white person who acknowledges the transparency phenomenon.

[3]

The Constitutional Requirement of Discriminatory Intent

T HE EQUAL PROTECTION Clause of the U.S. Constitution proscribes race discrimination, and accordingly is the provision to which one should look for legal redress when government engages in transparently white decisionmaking. Because transparency involves facially neutral criteria of decision, the specific doctrines of interest here are those that apply when government adopts a rule or makes a decision that is neutral on its face but carries racially disparate effects. This chapter describes the law currently governing constitutional disparate effects cases, concludes that it is inadequate to the task of challenging the transparency phenomenon, and proposes an alternative framework that might be more satisfactory.

The Requirement of Discriminatory Intent

The Fourteenth Amendment's Equal Protection Clause mandates that "No State shall . . . deny to any person within its jurisdiction the equal protection of the laws." By its terms, then, it applies to the individual states of the United States; the U.S. Supreme Court also has held that it applies, through the Fifth Amendment, to the federal government.[1] However, the constitutional guarantee of equal protection does not encompass the discriminatory conduct of private actors.

In 1954, in *Brown v. Board of Education*,[2] which held public school segregation unconstitutional, the U.S. Supreme Court ruled that race-specific government conduct disadvantaging blacks violates the Equal Protection Clause. However, it was not until 1976 that the Court made clear the circumstances under which a facially race-neutral government act or rule that has racially disparate effects would constitute a similar violation.

That year *Washington v. Davis*[3] made its way to the Supreme Court. *Davis* addressed the constitutionality of "Test 21," a written examination developed by the U.S. Civil Service Commission and administered to applicants for positions as officers in the Metropolitan Police Department of the District of Columbia. Two rejected black applicants argued that Test 21 was racially discriminatory in that its effect was to disqualify black applicants at approximately four times the rate of white applicants; the plaintiffs did not allege intentional discrimination. The challengers lost in the District Court but were, temporarily, more successful on appeal: The Court of Appeals for the D.C. Circuit concluded that the applicable constitutional standard should be borrowed from *Griggs v. Duke Power Co.*,[4] a 1971 Title VII case.[5] In *Griggs*, as it was then understood, the Supreme Court had ruled that disparate impact alone, without proof of discriminatory intent, would be adequate to support the finding of a statutory violation absent proof by the employer that the facially neutral criterion in question was related to job performance.[6] Though the District of Columbia petitioners challenged only the Court of Appeals' application of the *Griggs* approach, not the standard itself, the Supreme Court viewed the lower court's reliance on *Griggs* as plain error and set itself the task of correcting the mistake. The constitutional rule, the Court said, is that "the invidious quality of a law claimed to be racially discriminatory must ultimately be traced to a racially discriminatory purpose."[7]

In this context, "invidiousness" does not entail automatic invalidation. Proof that a statute with racially disparate effects was enacted because of a racially discriminatory motive would trigger "strict judicial scrutiny" of the enactment: The statute would be upheld if, and only if, the state could show that it had a "compelling" reason for adopting the legislation, and that the chosen means was "necessary" to achieve that objective. However, in race discrimination cases "strict scrutiny" generally is "fatal in fact."[8] Moreover, in the specific context of disparate effects cases it is especially unlikely that a challenged statute could survive strict scrutiny, because under the *Davis* rule strict scrutiny is applied only if the constitutional challenger already has shown that the legislation in question was adopted with a discriminatory intent, which is an impermissible purpose under any standard of review.

Justice White's opinion for the *Davis* Court rested the intent requirement principally on two arguments. First, the Court rejected a "group rights" approach to race discrimination. Notwithstanding that the failure rate for blacks as a group was higher than for whites, individual black applicants who failed the facially neutral test, the Court said, "could no more successfully claim that the test denied them equal protection than could white applicants who also failed."[9] Second, the Court expressed concern that a rule mandating strict scrutiny in all disparate effects cases would engage it in far-ranging economic redistribution. Such a rule "would be far reaching and would raise serious questions about, and perhaps invalidate, a whole range of tax, welfare, public service, regulatory, and licensing statutes that may be more burdensome to the poor and to the average black than to the more affluent white."[10]

The *Davis* rule is not limited to employment. In 1977 the Supreme Court elaborated the requirement of discriminatory intent in *Village of Arlington Heights v. Metropolitan Housing Development Corp.*[11] In that case the constitutional challenger was a developer who sought to build low- and moderate-income housing in the city of Arlington Heights, a suburb of Chicago; the city refused to alter the zoning classification of the property in question to permit the development. The Supreme Court accepted, at least for the sake of argument, the proposition that denying permission for the project would have a racially disproportionate impact, because minorities were overrepresented in the income groups that would be eligible for the new housing, relative to their proportion of the nearby population.[12] However, the Court concluded that the challengers had not demonstrated the presence of a discriminatory motive behind the decision not to rezone.[13]

Arlington Heights set forth relatively stringent requirements for proof of discriminatory intent, focusing on factors such as the specific sequence of events leading up to a challenged decision, departures from usual decisionmaking procedures, and departures from substantive factors normally taken into account in decisions of the sort under review.[14] However, in other settings the Court has articulated more relaxed standards for establishing discriminatory intent. In the context of jury selection, for example, the rule appears to be that a pattern of racially skewed outcomes plus a decisionmaking procedure that is "susceptible of abuse,"[15] or one that inherently provides an opportunity for discrimination, raises an inference of discriminatory intent.[16] With respect to voting rights, the rule seems even more lenient: A pattern of racially disparate effects plus "a showing that the jurisdiction has engaged in other types of discrimination in the past" seems adequate to establish discriminatory intent.[17] In short, the difficulty a constitutional challenger will face in attempting to prove that government acted with discriminatory intent varies with the sort of interest at stake: It is more difficult to accomplish with respect to housing and employment, and somewhat less difficult in the context of jury selection or voting rights.

Nevertheless, none of the discriminatory intent cases departs from a core conception of discriminatory intent, one that carries very strong connotations of conscious desire to do harm. In *Washington v. Davis* Justice Stevens joined the majority opinion, but also wrote separately to explain that in his view the distinction between discriminatory impact and discriminatory purpose was not as bright as it might at first seem, because "[f]requently the most probative evidence of intent will be objective evidence of what actually happened rather than evidence describing the subjective state of mind of the actor. For normally the actor is presumed to have intended the natural consequences of his deeds." [18] The Court addressed, and declined to adopt, Justice Stevens' position in *Personnel Administrator v. Feeney*, [19] a sex discrimination case. Feeney challenged a Massachusetts statute granting a nearly absolute preference in state civil service employment to veterans; she contended that because the class of veterans was overwhelmingly male, the preference inevitably and foreseeably operated to exclude women from the civil service. The Court rejected Feeney's argument, and with it Stevens' foreseeable effects approach, embracing instead the rule that discriminatory intent means that the decisionmaker chose a challenged facially neutral course of action " 'because of,' not merely 'in spite of,' its adverse effects upon an identifiable group." [20] This language very strongly suggests a model of conscious desire to cause the disadvantageous effects.

After *Davis* and *Feeney,* a state or federal criterion of decision that has disproportionate racial effects but is not shown to have been enacted "because of" those effects, triggers only rational basis review. This is a deferential mode of review, which requires only that the measure in question be "rationally related to a legitimate state interest." In effect, rational basis review affords the government's practices a presumption of constitutionality, and constitutional challenges resolved under the "rational basis" standard rarely succeed.

Very shortly after *Davis* was decided the Supreme Court

settled on an intermediate level of scrutiny in sex discrimination cases. This is a form of scrutiny that is neither deferential nor "fatal in fact"; it requires the state to show that a challenged measure is "substantially related to an important government objective."[21] Intermediate scrutiny has the virtue of engaging the reviewing court in an explicit examination of the constitutional values at stake in a particular case, but affords government a meaningful opportunity to justify a challenged practice.

Discriminatory Intent and Transparency

It is apparent that the requirement of discriminatory intent fails to provide any remedy at all for transparently white decisionmaking. Though transparently white criteria of decision inevitably produce racially disparate consequences, it would be inconsistent with the notion of "transparency" to suppose that those criteria of decision were chosen *because of* their racially skewed effects. Thus, by definition, it would be impossible to show discriminatory intent in a genuine case of transparently white decisionmaking.

The threshold requirement that the constitutional plaintiff prove discriminatory intent operates to draw a sharp distinction between facially neutral but unconsciously race-specific instances of white decisionmaking, on the one hand, and the deliberate use of race, whether overt or covert, on the other; only the latter is constitutionally impermissible. However, relying on a distinction among discriminators' states of mind seems a curious strategy for implementing the *Brown v.*

Board of Education principle that the use of race as a criterion of decision is what constitutes the constitutional harm, because race is equally the dispositive factor even when the process that brings it to bear is unconscious. Indeed, the discriminatory intent requirement appears more suited to drive the race specificity of white decisionmaking underground—out of whites' awareness—than to eradicate it altogether.[22] Nevertheless, the intent requirement might rest on either of two assumptions that, coupled with the perceived institutional costs of heightened scrutiny,* provide ostensible justification for the decision to disapprove only the purposeful use of race in government decisionmaking. These foundational assumptions are, first, that unconsciously race-specific decisionmaking is relatively rare, or, second, that the conscious use of race as a factor in decisionmaking is more blameworthy than its unconscious use.

The Belief in the Rarity of Unconscious Race Discrimination

The Supreme Court's decision to adopt a discriminatory intent rule that does not reach unconscious race-specific decisionmaking might rest on a belief that such discrimination is uncommon. Such a belief is, perhaps, the natural corollary of whites' widespread faith in the pervasiveness of race-neutrality. Whites seem to believe that most interactions and events

---

* "Heightened scrutiny" is a generic term that encompasses all forms of nondeferential judicial review—that is, both intermediate and strict scrutiny.

are untainted by racial considerations; we tend to see, for example, Klan and other overtly white supremacist attitudes as extreme, perhaps pathological, deviations from the (race-neutral) norm of white thought and behavior (as if white supremacist attitudes can be comprehended in complete isolation from the culture in which they are embedded). Similarly, whites tend to adopt the "things are getting better" story of race relations, which allows us to suppose that our unfortunate history of socially approved race discrimination is largely behind us. This nexus of white confidence in race neutrality might dictate that the law should treat the unconscious use of nonobviously race-specific criteria of decision as nothing more than the occasional deviation from the prevailing practice of race-neutral government decisionmaking. From this perspective, given that significant institutional costs are associated with judicial intervention,** unconscious race specificity seems too rare to justify heightened review.

The transparency phenomenon provides two arguments against the view that unconscious race specificity is unusual. At minimum, it counsels that we hesitate to acquiesce in any view that accepts race neutrality at face value, whether as a matter of fact or of frequency of occurrence. Second, transparency supports the stronger, affirmative argument that unconscious race-specific decisionmaking is so common that it is in fact the norm for white decisionmakers.

The belief that race-neutral decisionmaking is relatively common and unconsciously race-specific decisionmaking rel-

---

** These institutional costs are examined at some length in chapter 4.

atively uncommon stands analytically distinct from the belief that any particular instance of facially neutral decisionmaking is in fact what it seems. Even if the unconscious use of race were extremely rare, whites still could misperceive the true character of every one of the few instances in which race in fact was a factor in the decision. Conversely, the fact that whites frequently are unaware of the white-specific factors that may be used in white decisionmaking does not dictate one conclusion or another regarding the frequency with which such factors actually are employed. This analytic distinction notwithstanding, transparency counsels skepticism with respect to the frequency of race-neutral decisionmaking as well.

Because the transparency phenomenon creates a risk that whites will misapprehend the race-specific nature of apparently race-neutral decisionmaking, it simultaneously creates a risk that we will systematically underestimate the incidence of such decisionmaking. Each circumstance in which we fail to perceive accurately the racial content of our decisions contributes to the overall perception that race neutrality is the more common way of doing business. Thus, even though the conclusion that race specificity is the norm does not necessarily follow from transparency alone, we ought to adopt a healthy skepticism toward, rather than a blind faith in the pervasiveness of, race neutrality, if we wish to be able to assess more accurately the role of race in white decisionmaking.

Transparency also lends support to the stronger position that unconscious race-specific decisionmaking is so common that it is in fact the normal mode of white decisionmaking.

This argument rests in part on an analysis of the outcomes of discretionary white decisionmaking. Numerous studies indicate that whites receive more favorable treatment than blacks in virtually every area of social interaction.[23] The weight of the evidence supports the conclusion that race affects whites' discretionary decisionmaking in areas as diverse as hiring and performance evaluations in employment settings;[24] mortgage lending, insurance redlining, and retail bargaining;[25] psychiatric diagnoses;[26] responses to patient violence in mental institutions;[27] and virtually every stage in the criminal law process: arrest,[28] the decision to charge,[29] imprisonment,[30] and capital sentencing.[31]

Studies of the impact of race on white decisionmaking nearly always explain disparate race effects by focusing on negative assessments of, or undesirable outcomes for, nonwhites, rather than positive results for whites. That is, they adopt a conceptual framework in which unconscious race discrimination tends to be associated with prejudice or stereotyping rather than transparency. At the same time, each of the studies cited above controls the data for race-neutral variables, so that the influence of race on the decisionmaking process can be assessed in isolation from other factors. The transparency phenomenon suggests that the selected independent variables may in fact be transparently white-specific. When they are, additional race effects, though different in kind from those conceptualized by the researchers, are present as well.

In sum, the social science literature indicates that race impacts most white decisionmaking most of the time, and the researchers' own susceptibility to transparency suggests that unconscious discrimination may be even more prevalent than the studies acknowledge. It follows that faith in the commonality of race-neutral decisionmaking is a component of white race consciousness that lacks any solid empirical support.

The Belief That Conscious Discrimination Is More Blameworthy Than Unconscious Discrimination

A second foundational belief that might be proffered to justify the line drawn by the discriminatory intent rule is that the conscious use of race-specific criteria of decision is more blameworthy than the unconscious use of race. That view is consistent with the familiar legal principle that conduct intended to cause a specified harmful result is more blameworthy than conduct that causes the same harm inadvertently. In other words, the law commonly recognizes degrees of culpability associated with different states of mind. In the criminal law, for example, the Model Penal Code distinguishes, and ranks hierarchically, four kinds of culpability, based on acts done purposely, knowingly, recklessly, or negligently.[32] By analogy, if the harm of race discrimination lies in the use of race as a criterion of decision, the levels-of-culpability model would seem to suggest that the conscious or purposeful use of race as a criterion of decision should be deemed more blameworthy than the unconscious use of race.

In the *Washington v. Davis* opinion, the Supreme Court implicitly framed the issue as whether a showing of a racially disparate impact would trigger strict scrutiny or rational basis review. Thus, adopting the rule that strict scrutiny would apply only upon proof of discriminatory intent meant that government actions reflecting only unconscious race discrimination—in which discriminatory intent is absent—would enjoy the presumption of constitutionality associated with rational basis review. To whatever extent any constitutional doctrine is founded on, or is designed to reflect, a conception of moral blameworthiness, the clear implication is that unconscious racism is not merely less blameworthy than its purposeful counterpart, but is not blameworthy at all.

Clearly, legal rules do not determine the moral status of the conduct they proscribe or permit. For example, the "no duty to rescue" rule receives nearly universal criticism for its failure to impose liability for conduct commonly thought to be morally blameworthy.[33] On the other hand, legal doctrines do carry normative messages, more insistently in some contexts than in others. We ought to take the normative dimension of the discriminatory intent rule quite seriously for at least two reasons.

First, the Supreme Court itself has emphasized the normative dimension of its constitutional liability rules by increasingly crafting "state of mind" requirements reminiscent of the discourse of criminal liability. In addition to the *Washington v. Davis* rule itself, the Court has held that neither an Eighth Amendment nor a Due Process violation may be predicated on negligent conduct alone,[34] has formulated good faith exceptions to the exclusionary rule and to the constitutional guarantee of a criminal defendant's access to evidence,[35] and has fashioned a qualified immunity doctrine that partially insulates government actors from section 1983[36] and *Bivens*[37] liability.[38] Even though these requirements of intent or "bad faith" tend to be tested by objective standards, and therefore are not literally "state of mind" requirements, the larger message is that there is a culpability element to (some) constitutional violations, which strengthens the analogy to criminal conduct.

Second, whites share no apparent consensus concerning the morality of unconscious race discrimination. Indeed, the transparency phenomenon suggests that no such consensus is attainable at present because unconscious discrimination that takes the form of transparently white-specific criteria of decision is by definition unseen by the white discriminator. Against this background, the manner in which the Court chooses to address unconscious discrimination inevitably will have a powerful normative effect, either to legitimate or to challenge accepted but unexamined white ways of thinking about race. The message that unconscious discrimination, if it exists, is not (very) blameworthy makes it more likely that whites will continue to deny the existence of unconscious discrimination.

In eschewing heightened scrutiny for racially disparate effects absent proof of discriminatory intent, the Court sends two messages that operate to legitimate unconscious race discrimination. First, the discriminatory intent rule recreates transparency at the level of constitutional doctrine, for it affords a presumption of race neutrality to facially neutral criteria of decision without regard to the possibility that those criteria in fact reflect white-specific characteristics, attitudes, or experiences. The rule tends to reassure whites that all is well so long as we avoid the conscious use of race-specific bases for decision.

The requirement of discriminatory intent also legitimates

unconscious race discrimination by reinforcing a popular white story about progress in race relations. The central theme of this story is that our society has an unfortunate history of race discrimination that is largely behind us. In the past, the story goes, some unenlightened individuals practiced slavery and other forms of overt oppression of black people, but the belief in the inferiority of blacks upon which these practices were premised has almost entirely disappeared today. We, aside from the exceptional few who remain out of step with the times, think of blacks as the equals of whites and thus no longer accept race as a permissible basis for different treatment. The Court's discriminatory intent rule contributes to this dominant story insofar as it treats as blameworthy the form of race discrimination most common in the past but refuses to regard with suspicion the unconscious discrimination that is at least as significant a cause of the oppression of black people today.

Transparency-Conscious Scrutiny

I now set forth a constitutional disparate impact rule designed to address the consequences of the transparency phenomenon as it affects government decisionmaking. I recognize that not all government actions that arguably violate the Equal Protection Clause are products of transparency, and I emphasize that this proposal does not foreclose finding some government decisions unconstitutional because motivated by racial animus. Other conduct might properly be invalidated because animated by racial stereotyping. Accordingly, the disparate impact rule I propose would be only one piece in a complete equal protection jurisprudence. This proposal aims specifically at government decisions that carry racially disparate consequences and likely would not have been adopted but for the transparency phenomenon.

In outline, the proposed rule calls for heightened scrutiny of governmental criteria of decision that have racially disparate effects. First, the constitutional challenger must show that a facially neutral criterion of decision has a disproportionate racial impact. Once disparate impact is proven, government must articulate the purposes behind the challenged rule of decision. The reviewing court ought to interpret government's asserted purpose(s) in as pluralist a manner as possible, but government has the option of resisting that interpretation in favor of an assimilationist construction of its goals. In that event, government will bear a burden of justification similar to that imposed under traditional intermediate scrutiny. Finally, whether governmental purposes are construed pluralistically or in an assimilationist manner, the constitutional challenger has the obligation to bring forward alternative means of achieving government's goals. Government must implement the challenger's proposals unless it can demonstrate that those alternatives provide less effective means of implementing its goals than the criteria of decision originally employed.

The thoroughly skeptical white decisionmaker regards all facially neutral criteria of decision as presumptively white-specific; the existence of racially disparate effects only confirms what his skepticism already counsels. Thus, the individual decisionmaker who takes transparency seriously has no need for a rule that treats facially neutral criteria of decision with racially disparate effects differently from facially neutral criteria in general. However, that stance is unworkable as a constitutional rule because it would require heightened judicial scrutiny of virtually every governmental decision. A rule that requires a showing of disparate effects as a predicate for heightened scrutiny is a satisfactory alternative because it provides for judicial intervention whenever the presumed transparency phenomenon has produced concrete racial consequences.

Because it is the issue that triggers heightened scrutiny, the constitutional challenger must demonstrate the existence of racially disproportionate effects. However, the history of Title VII disparate impact litigation reveals a potential hazard. As is the case under the constitutional rule proposed here, a Title VII plaintiff's proof of disparate impact alone places a burden of justification on the defendant; in the Title VII context the ensuing evidentiary warfare has been intense and highly technical.[39] While the *Washington v. Davis* rule provides no similar incentive for constitutional defendants to search out ways to contest plaintiffs' factual claims of disparate effects (because plaintiffs already bear the burden of proving discriminatory intent), the proposed rule, mandating heightened scrutiny upon disproportionate effects alone, clearly carries the potential for similar litigation strategies.

Accordingly, the proposed rule anticipates the need for evidentiary guidelines concerning proof of adverse effects, and it permits the constitutional challenger to make such a demonstration by relying on a statistical disparity between the racial composition of the group selected by the challenged criteria of decision and that of the general population. That is, the challenger need show only that the criterion in question occurs, or is based on a characteristic that occurs, differentially across races.*** This a relatively broad approach to the question of proof of disparate effects; it effectively requires government to justify its practices regardless of who or what caused a given disparity. This is a desirable feature of the proposed rule. Mandating heightened scrutiny in more, rather than fewer, cases plausibly characterized as exhibiting disparate effects is consistent with the skepticism regarding race neutrality awakened by consciousness of the transparency phenomenon: If we are to ferret out transparently white-specific criteria of decision, government should bear the task of justification more rather than less frequently.

Once the constitutional challenger has proved the existence of racially disparate effects, government should have to articulate the purpose or goal of the challenged criteria. This simply assures that the challenger will not be required to guess at government's policies or purposes. However, transparency can infect government's purposes as readily as it can affect chosen means, so the interpretation of government's articulated purpose is critical.

Heightened, transparency-conscious scrutiny of governmental purposes requires the reviewing court to construe

---

*** This proposal is functionally equivalent to the way disparate impact would be established under the "foreseeable effects" approach to Title VII set forth in chapter 5. That chapter also includes discussion of many of the technical issues that have arisen in Title VII disparate impact cases.

those purposes in a manner that does not perpetuate the covert imposition of white norms. One way to avoid the reintroduction of transparency is for courts to interpret government's goals in as culturally pluralist a manner as possible. That is, the reviewing court should inquire whether and to what extent government's articulated goal, viewed at an appropriate level of generality, may be construed to encompass objectives that need not be understood as white-specific. For example, in *Fragante v. City & County of Honolulu*[40] a Filipino job applicant who achieved the highest score on the applicable civil service examination was rejected for a position as a clerk at the Department of Motor Vehicles because he spoke English with a heavy Filipino accent. Had the case been litigated as a constitutional challenge to a facially neutral rule requiring clerks to speak "unaccented" English, the government most likely would have identified effective communication with the public as the purpose behind the rule.

The transparency of the norm of "unaccented" speech should be obvious. Fragante's speech was perceived as "difficult" by individuals who, consciously or unconsciously, preferred the speech of people with accents more nearly like that of white Americans.[41] This case also illustrates the temptation for government to attempt to justify a transparently white criterion of decision with an equally white-specific purpose. From that perspective, the central problem of the case is the suppressed whiteness of the notion of "effective communication" with the public, government's proffered "legitimate, nondiscriminatory reason."

Under the disparate impact analysis proposed here, a reviewing court ought to construe government's purpose, if possible, in a manner that would not advantage whites. That is, the court would have to presume the "public" to be a diverse community and give "effective communication" the broadest possible reading. If the court unconsciously interpreted "effective communication" to mean "effective communication with whites," it would have reintroduced transparency in a manner that would defeat the underlying goals of heightened scrutiny.

On the other hand, government ought to have the option of insisting on a construction of its purpose that is white-specific, when it has good reasons for doing so. On occasion, context may provide a good reason: If, for example, all or nearly all of the persons with whom Mr. Fragante would come into contact were in fact white, government should be permitted to seek "effective communication" with that group, even if its purpose is thus effectively white-specific. However, a rule of general applicability would require a more thorough evaluation of government's goals. Suppose government argued that "effective communication" should be construed in a white-specific manner for the sake of uniformity and that a white norm had been adopted because whites are the dominant group in this society. At this stage the reviewing court would revert to a more traditional form of scrutiny, balancing government's interest in uniformity and whiteness against the burden the adoption of a white-specific rule would place on nonwhites. To prevail under this "mid-level" scrutiny, government's chosen purpose must be "important." At minimum, an asserted interest in administrative convenience would not be sufficient.[42]

Once the question of purpose has been settled, whether in

an assimilationist or a pluralist manner, the challenger must introduce means of achieving that purpose that do not disproportionately disadvantage nonwhites. In the *Fragante* situation the challenger might propose one or more functional tests for "effective communication with the public" that would measure, for example, the actual ability of the relevant set of listeners to comprehend Mr. Fragante's speech. This "relevant set" of listeners would be determined by the court's construction of the governmental purpose. An assimilationist interpretation would define the relevant group as being completely or essentially white; a pluralist interpretation would envision a more diverse audience. In either case, the challenger would have the opportunity to propose alternative criteria of selection that would effectuate government's goal. The challenger should be allowed at this stage to propose measures that would operate to the advantage of nonwhite applicants, as well as criteria of selection that would be racially neutral in effect.

Finally, government must show that the challenger's proposed alternative(s) would be less effective in achieving its purpose, as interpreted by the court, than the criteria of decision employed by the government. If government fails to carry its burden here, it will be required to employ the challenger's criteria of decision either as a substitute for, or in parallel with, the criteria previously in use. In the abstract, parallel use of alternative criteria of decision would be preferable in cases in which the challenger's proposed criteria of selection operate to advantage nonwhites, and substitution would be appropriate if the proffered alternative had racially neutral effects. For example, in the *Fragante* scenario, a functional, actual-ability-to-be-understood test would not systematically advantage nonwhites over whites, and so substitution of that test for the hypothesized requirement of "unaccented" speech would be preferable.

Like the traditional forms of heightened scrutiny employed in equal protection analysis, the disparate impact rule proposed here places increased burdens of justification on government with respect both to its purposes and its means, but the rule does so with special attention to the transparency phenomenon. Thus, where traditional heightened review requires that government's purpose be unusually weighty (and, arguably, that it be contemporaneous with the challenged rule or decision and adequately supported in fact), transparency-conscious scrutiny requires government to articulate purposes that are neither overtly nor transparently white-specific. Government may impose norms that are effectively white, but it must announce its choice candidly, and it must bear a substantial burden of justification when it wishes to do so. Traditional heightened scrutiny then demands a sufficiently tight "fit" between government's goal and its chosen means; the proposed rule requires the use of alternative criteria of decision that have no racially disparate impact whenever doing so will not negatively affect government's permissible purposes.

The *Washington v. Davis* facts provide another, more challenging application of the proposed rule. The *Davis* facts are analyzed here as raising a problem of dialect, while *Fragante* concerned accent discrimination. A dialect is a variant of a language; accent refers to manner of pronunciation. One can speak any dialect in a variety of accents. In particular, the dialect known as "standard" English can be spoken with a Filipino accent, an African American accent, or the accent known as "General American." [43] The analysis that follows assumes, for the sake of discussion, that at least some of the unsuccessful *Davis* applicants were more proficient in the dialect known as Black English (sometimes labeled "Ebonics") than in "standard" (White) English. In this respect, I depart from the more common hypothesis that the difficulties experienced by the actual *Davis* plaintiffs had been the result of inferior, segregated education. Black English is a fully developed language. [44] My intuition is that there is a difference between accent and dialect here: Whites are more willing to tolerate and accommodate (some) accent pluralism than we are dialect variation.

In *Washington v. Davis* the challenged criterion of decision was "Test 21," a written test of "verbal ability, vocabulary, reading and comprehension." Test 21 had an undisputed disparate racial impact: Black applicants failed it at four times the rate of white applicants. Government's articulated purpose was "modestly to upgrade the communicative abilities of its employees . . . particularly where the job requires special ability to communicate orally and in writing." [45]

At the stage of purpose analysis, the reviewing court would begin with the presumption that government had not set out to foster in all its police officers only the "communicative abilities" of white persons, though government could, if it wished, make the case that that was precisely what it had intended. The underlying agenda of this sort of purpose review is to require government to clarify its goals, and concomitantly to expose transparently white-specific governmental purposes. If government was seeking officer-candidates able to communicate effectively with a diverse—in Washington, D.C., a majority black—public, a pluralist interpretation of its purpose would be most appropriate. On the other hand, if government was pursuing a degree of language standardization, say with the intent to "professionalize" the police department, it would be evident that "professionalization" had been implicitly defined by reference to white norms, and so further justification of that goal, and of the white language standard it incorporates, would be in order.[46] Judge Robb, who dissented from the Court of Appeals decision that held Test 21 unconstitutional, articulated government's best case for language standardization:

[M]odern law enforcement is a highly skilled professional service. In school and thereafter in practice a policeman must learn and understand intricate procedures. He must understand a myriad of regulations, statutes and judicial rulings, and he will be called upon to apply them in his daily work.

He must be able to present relevant facts in literate, clear and precise reports. When he testifies in court he must be articulate. He cannot achieve these goals unless he has a basic understanding of the English language and the meaning of words and the ability to perceive the import of written sentences.[47]

In short, police officers must be able to comprehend and to speak White English because it is the language of law and the courtroom.

Whether language standardization constitutes an "important" government purpose in this context is a close question. Arguably, language standardization in the police force (and in the courts, and government generally) implicates more than mere "administrative convenience." My own sense is that a reviewing court would deem it "important"; if so, it would survive judicial scrutiny under the proposed rule. At issue is the ability of the white majority to govern itself in its own language, and, if there is going to be a limit to cultural pluralism anywhere, it will most likely be located at or near the seat of government. Put somewhat more positively, the majority white government is entitled to require that the officers it engages to enforce the law are able to comprehend its commands. On the other hand, it also can be said that government has a duty to articulate its commands in ways that are comprehensible to its citizens; hence the conclusion that this is a close question.

In whatever manner government's purpose is finally construed, the challengers may then formulate and propose alternative means of achieving government's goals that they believe will not disadvantage black applicants. If, for example, communication with the (racially mixed) public was the sought-after skill, the challengers might come up with a "Test 22" that would measure language skills appropriate to one or more nonwhite segments of the community. They might then propose that all applicants be required to achieve a minimum combined score on Test 21 and "Test 22," or to receive some minimum score on either test.

Envisioning pluralist means of implementing a government goal that has been given a monocultural interpretation is more difficult. Perhaps the ingenious challenger could identify some sort of language acquisition test that would select applicants who could be expected to have a relatively easy time acquiring the required skill in "standard" English; but perhaps no such test is available. If none is, heightened scrutiny would have functioned to identify an area of government decisionmaking in which assimilationism is permissible. The increase in candor associated with acknowledging the whiteness of formerly transparent white norms would in itself constitute an advance in race relations.

If the challengers propose alternative selection criteria, government must demonstrate that adoption of the proposed alternative to the sole use of Test 21 would impede its search for officers with "upgraded communicative abilities," as construed at the stage of purpose analysis. If it cannot sustain that burden, government must adopt the challengers' recommendations. Continued use of Test 21 alone would, under those circumstances, constitute an unjustifiable refusal to take transparency seriously.

The deeper design of the proposed rule is to foster constructive dialogue concerning the necessity and appropriateness of assimilationist governmental purposes and means. The transparency phenomenon means that blacks evaluated under "facially neutral" norms in fact often face a choice between assimilation and exclusion. The proposed rule is intended to counteract the assimilationist force of transparency and to require government to confront the possibility of greater openness to cultural diversity in the formulation of public policy and the exercise of governmental power. At the same time, the constitutional challenger becomes responsible for proposing alternative means of achieving government's articulated goals. This requirement operates to relieve a white-controlled government of some of the burden of diversification; it does not require whites suddenly to be able to envision remedies for a phenomenon that has too often escaped our awareness altogether. There is a danger here of permitting white decisionmakers to evade responsibility for transparency, because the burden is on challengers to propose alternatives to facially neutral but white-specific criteria of decision. White people should not always rely on blacks to explain racism to us.[48] Nevertheless, in the interest of setting forth a proposal that is within whites' reach, I settled on the requirement that nonwhites who challenge transparently white-specific governmental criteria of decision must take an active role in reformulating them.

[4]

Constitutional Qualms

I BELIEVE THE PROPOSAL set forth in chapter 3 is adoptable, in the sense that it is consistent with Equal Protection principles and with what we know about transparently white decisionmaking, the problem it was designed to address. However, some constitutional scholars would disagree with the first of those propositions, and in addition might argue that this proposal is inconsistent with a principle of judicial restraint that today affects virtually all constitutional analysis. This chapter addresses in turn these two sources of resistance to the proposed transparency-conscious rule.

The Meaning of Equal Protection

The proposed rule clearly abandons the colorblindness principle, which disapproves any use of a race-specific criterion of decision, no matter what the race of the decisionmaker or of the persons respectively advantaged or burdened by that criterion. First, the proposed rule is founded on the presumption that facially neutral criteria of decision employed by white decisionmakers are in fact race-specific; the rule at least challenges the assumption of the colorblindness perspective that such a thing as a racially neutral criterion of decision is possible. Second, the rule permits government to take responsibility for disparate racial effects by adopting parallel race-conscious criteria of decision in appropriate instances. Finally, though the proposed rule does resemble colorblindness insofar as it mandates heightened scrutiny in the interest of mitigating the race-based effects of some covertly race-specific criteria of decision, it does so only when those effects flow from transparently white-specific bases of decision. That is, the rule contemplates heightened judicial scrutiny only when ostensibly neutral criteria formulated or deployed by white governmental decisionmakers operate to disadvantage nonwhites. It is not symmetrical; heightened scrutiny is not appropriate when black governmental decisionmakers formulate and apply facially neutral criteria that negatively impact whites.

A transparency-conscious disparate impact rule should not be symmetrical because transparency itself is a white-specific phenomenon. In our society only whites have the social power that renders our point of view perspectiveless, that elevates our expectations to the status of "neutral" norms, and that permits us to see ourselves and our race-specific characteristics as raceless. Assuming there are, or can be, meaningful instances in which nonwhites gain the power to formulate as well as to apply governmental rules of decision, the existence of any disparate negative effect on whites would trigger at minimum an immediate inquiry, by whites, into the possible racial components of such facially neutral rules. Thus, in this society, nonwhite decisionmaking never benefits from transparency.

Nevertheless, colorblindness is such a powerful norm that many will see its abandonment as a serious defect of the proposed rule. Further reflection will demonstrate, however, that colorblindness is a highly problematic constitutional principle. Justice Scalia, the strictest adherent to the color-blindness principle currently on the Supreme Court, staked out his position in the words of Alexander Bickel: "The lesson of the great decisions of the Supreme Court and the lesson of contemporary history have been the same for at least a generation: discrimination on the basis of race is illegal, immoral, unconstitutional, inherently wrong, and destructive of democratic society."[1] I address in turn the claims that colorblindness is an established constitutional principle, that it is morally self-evident, and that it is instrumental to the attainment of racial justice.

The available evidence suggests that its framers did not understand the Fourteenth Amendment to constitutionalize an abstract colorblindness principle. First, the series of race-conscious Freedmen's Bureau Acts adopted in the same period as the Fourteenth Amendment supports the conclusion that the framers did not oppose race-conscious legislation per se.[2] However, the argument that those Acts were directed exclusively at aiding the actual victims of prior discrimination dilutes the inference that the framers supported race-conscious measures.[3] The stronger case against the colorblindness interpretation rests, ironically, on the work of

Alexander Bickel, who reached the conclusion that the framers did not intend to outlaw segregated public education, antimiscegenation laws, or the exclusion of blacks from jury service and the vote.[4] Bickel concluded that the framers left open the question of giving "greater protection" than the Civil Rights Act of 1866, which for him would have meant extending the prohibition against race-conscious measures, "to be decided another day."[5] The colorblindness principle has become entrenched in constitutional doctrine, but rather gradually. As a matter of constitutional precedent, it is quite the new arrival on the block.[6]

Contemporary commentators saw no unequivocal commitment to colorblindness in *Brown v. Board of Education,*[7] though some argued that the series of per curiam decisions that followed it compelled the conclusion that *Brown* rested on colorblindness after all.[8] However, subsequent desegregation decisions cut the other way; they tended to rely on racial balancing as a proxy for desegregation and on occasion suggested that race-conscious measures might be permissible outside the remedial context.[9] Though the Court did adopt one rule embodying the colorblindness perspective in 1976— the requirement of discriminatory intent itself—it declined to do the same in the more controversial context of race-specific affirmative action when opportunities arose in 1974[10] and 1978.[11] The Court did not settle on an explicit doctrine requiring strict scrutiny of all race-specific measures until 1989.[12]

The evolution of the role of colorblindness in Equal Protection discourse is enlightening. Colorblindness was not in itself especially controversial in the early post-*Brown* era. Its significance lay in its potential to resolve a process-theoretical difficulty Herbert Wechsler had understood *Brown* to pose: In his view, *Brown* had failed to articulate a "neutral principle" supporting its holding.[13] Some commentators saw colorblindness as such a principle. As one might expect, the colorblindness principle became an item of contention in its own right as the debate over affirmative action heated up. However, it shed its ties to process theory at the same time, largely because process theory, as refined by John Ely, found another approach to, and resolution of, the question of affirmative action: Strict scrutiny is not appropriate when the white majority decides to favor nonwhites at its own expense.[14] Increasingly, colorblindness was defended in moral and substantive terms, featuring, for example, instrumental arguments that race-conscious measures would ultimately exacerbate racial tensions or that they inevitably stigmatize blacks.[15] This shift in theoretical perspective, from the search for "neutrality" to the avowedly substantive, coincided, of course, with the conceptualization of the "innocent" white "victim" of affirmative action.[16] The current preeminence of the colorblindness principle in constitutional discourse thus appears, at least in part, attributable to its utility in defending white privilege.

Turning from the legal to the moral realm, the foundation of colorblindness seems to lie in its enormous intuitive appeal. To "judge a person by the color of his skin" just seems wrong.[17] This moral insight may be the visceral rejection of its equally visceral opposite, the tendency of human beings to react negatively to persons of a different color than themselves. However, distributive racial justice has at least as strong a claim to center stage as a guiding moral principle in the abstract, and, I would argue, emerges as the compelling lodestar for moral conduct in a society such as this one, with a history of slavery, apartheid, and ongoing racial oppression.

The colorblindness principle may also appear morally desirable by virtue of its relation to the liberal value of individual autonomy. Colorblindness often is seen as an expression of autonomy, which requires in part that persons not be held responsible or judged for personal characteristics not within their own control. Individuals ought to reap the fruits of their own industry, but they ought neither to benefit nor to be disadvantaged because of characteristics like race or gender that are a matter of birth.

However, colorblindness is at best a paradoxical means of implementing autonomy values. On the one hand, autonomy is not served when the individual is pigeonholed by race; certainly the whole person is much more than the color of her skin. On the other hand, individual autonomy ought to include the power of self-definition, the ability to make fundamental value choices and to select life strategies to implement them. Such choices are not unbounded; for many individuals, to be oneself is to share in the cultural values of a community to which one belongs by birth. Thus, for example, for many black people embracing blackness as an explicit and positive aspect of personal identity is an essential component in the process of self-definition.[18]

Here again the *Washington v. Davis* facts are illustrative. Some black applicants almost certainly had grown up and continued to live in black neighborhoods in which Black

English was the primary spoken dialect, and it was equally likely that some of those would prefer to use that dialect on the job as well. Test 21, however, measured proficiency in "standard" (White) English and likely signaled the intent of the police department to require the use of White English in the workplace. Even the Black English speakers who passed Test 21 must have experienced some loss, or displacement, of self on the job; the unsuccessful test takers essentially were told that they could not occupy the powerful post of police officer if they remained monolingual in Black English.

Proponents of the existing requirement of discriminatory intent appear to believe that individual autonomy is served when decisionmakers "ignore" the race of those affected by their decisions, but the transparency phenomenon, which suggests that colorblindness may operate instead as a vehicle for the unthinking imposition of white norms and expectations, belies that view. The proposed rule takes a broader view of personal autonomy and takes seriously the centrality of race to many individuals' self-definition. For those who have to choose between the language, customs, hairstyle, dress, or lifestyle of their own community and a desirable job or other governmental benefit, the autonomy costs of transparently white norms are considerable.

The final category of arguments purporting to support the colorblindness principle may be characterized, loosely, as exemplifying antisubordinative concerns. Race consciousness—the explicit use of racial classifications as a means of disadvantaging nonwhites—has been the primary vehicle of racial subordination until quite recently.[19] The ideology of opposition to racial hierarchy evolved in reaction to the specific forms in which racial oppression had manifested itself. Rejecting racial distinctions seemed the natural avenue to reversing that history of oppression and achieving racial justice, especially during the "Second Reconstruction" of the 1950s and 1960s; colorblindness appeared to be the exact antithesis of the form of race consciousness that had been the root cause of racial subordination.[20] If "color" had marked an individual as inferior, then the refusal to recognize "color" would be the way to elevate him to equal status with whites. In effect, colorblindness became the rule-like proxy for an underlying, historically based antisubordination principle.[21]

The problem with the colorblindness principle as a strategy for achieving racial justice is that it has not been effective outside the social context in which it arose. Like all rules, colorblindness is both over- and underinclusive with respect to the underlying policy—antisubordination—it is intended to implement. It is underinclusive because the explicit use of racial classifications is no longer the principal vehicle of racial oppression; structural and institutional racism, of the sort illustrated by the transparency phenomenon, now are the predominant causes of blacks' continued inability to thrive in this society. Colorblindness is overinclusive insofar as it regards the explicit use of racial classifications to advantage blacks as equally blameworthy as the historical use of such classifications to disadvantage them. In each respect colorblindness fails to implement racial justice; that it is a failed social policy is evident from the statistics revealing that blacks are scarcely better off today than they were before this ideology took hold in the 1950s and 1960s.[22]

Whites who wish to implement the goal of racial justice should give up the colorblindness principle in favor of a functional analysis of proposed means of achieving those ends. The proposed rule offers a better prospect for achieving racial equity because it permits nonwhites to engage white-controlled government in a dialogue concerning the scope of government's goals and the range of means that might be effective in attaining them. It requires government to define its goals in ways that do not systematically favor whites, and it also requires government to utilize diverse means of achieving its goals whenever possible. Unlike the inflexible, acontextual, and ahistorical colorblindness principle, the proposed rule offers the opportunity for government to take responsibility for racial justice.

The Principle of Judicial Restraint

This tradition holds that the judiciary ought to defer to legislative policy choices, absent special justification for judicial intervention. For the most part, it can be traced to reaction against the Supreme Court's performance during the *Lochner* era, a period of unparalleled judicial activism between 1899 and 1937 during which the Court invalidated almost two hundred state and federal statutes and regulations.[23] The Court's activist stance generated intense political and intellectual opposition. Politically, the Court's invalidation of key New Deal legislation threatened emerging Roosevelt administration policies.[24] This aspect of the problem was resolved in relatively short order, however. The "switch-in-time"[25] that signaled the close of the *Lochner* era was followed by a series of Roosevelt appointments[26] that effectively foreclosed any possible resurgence of the *Lochner* approach.

On the intellectual front, two distinct accounts of the errors of the Court's *Lochner* era jurisprudence emerged. One challenged the substantive premises on which the decisions of that period had rested, with particular emphasis on the Court's failure to engage in a meaningful analysis of existing unequal distributions of wealth and power.[27] The second criticism was an institutional one: The Court should not have substituted its judgment for that of the legislature with regard to controversial value choices.[28] The latter understanding of the *Lochner* era has come to dominate constitutional theory and doctrine.[29]

The institutional criticism of the *Lochner* Court drew upon a preexisting line of arguments advocating judicial restraint. In 1893, James B. Thayer argued in his influential paper *The Origin and Scope of the American Doctrine of Constitutional Law*[30] that courts should exercise the power of judicial review only "when those who have the right to make laws have not merely made a mistake regarding constitutionality, but have made a very clear one,—so clear that it is not open to rational question."[31] In Thayer's view, the constitutional text is open to a variety of interpretations. While each of the political branches has an obligation to make a judgment concerning the constitutionality of its own behavior, the coordinate branches of government would be unable to function together unless each respected the authority of the others to act upon reasonable interpretations of their constitutional mandates. Therefore, a legislative judgment that a particular enactment is constitutional is entitled to judicial respect unless the legislature's assessment is clearly erroneous. In addition, Thayer suggested that legislatures were more competent than courts to make policy, and that too frequent invalidation of legislative acts might undermine the legislature's will to engage seriously with "questions of justice and right." [32]

Thayer's principle of judicial restraint exerted a profound influence on the judicial philosophies of Justices Holmes, Brandeis, and Frankfurter.[33] Their written opinions at times reflected an additional argument in favor of judicial restraint: the image of the judiciary as a "nondemocratic" institution.[34] For example, in 1949 Justice Frankfurter contended that:

In the day-to-day working of our democracy it is vital that the power of the non-democratic organ of our Government be exercised with rigorous self-restraint. Because the powers exercised by this Court are inherently oligarchic, Jefferson all of his life thought of the Court as "an irresponsible body" and "independent of the nation itself." The Court is not saved from being oligarchic because it professes to act in the service of humane ends.[35]

This version of the principle of restraint has been developed more fully in the academic literature. In Alexander Bickel's classic statement, for instance, the power of judicial review should be exercised with caution because of the "counter-majoritarian" character of the judiciary: "When the Supreme Court declares unconstitutional a legislative act or the action of an elected executive, it thwarts the will of representatives of the actual people of the here and now; it exercises control, not in behalf of the prevailing majority, but against it." [36]

Taken together, these arguments constitute a case for judicial restraint that dominates the landscapes of mainstream constitutional theory and doctrine to this day. In both realms, advocates of judicial review generally perceive a need to confront and overcome the "legitimacy" question.[37] From this perspective, constitutional analysis begins with a presumption of legislative regularity: Some special circumstance is required to validate a stance other than judicial deference to the legislature's judgment. Doctrinally, this "deference-and-departure" framework finds its expression in the notion of different "levels" of review. Nondeferential judicial review is generally labeled "heightened scrutiny," a term that underscores its status as a departure from the norm.

This concern over—some might say preoccupation with—the legitimacy of judicial review finds doctrinal expression in at least three aspects of race discrimination law.[38] First, it exerts pressure in the direction of society's mainstream or "traditional" values. In the context of race discrimination law, heightened scrutiny can be expected to be more palatable if it targets generally recognized forms of discrimination, than if it aims at redressing less widely acknowledged ones.

The discriminatory intent requirement adopted in *Washington v. Davis* diverged from the Court's contemporaneous interpretation of Title VII. In *Griggs v. Duke Power Co.*,[39] the Court had ruled that a showing of racially disparate effects alone, without proof of discriminatory intent, would be sufficient to support the finding of a Title VII statutory violation absent proof by the defendant that the facially neutral criterion at issue was related to job performance. The Court of Appeals in *Davis* had applied the *Griggs* standard in the constitutional context,[40] but this approach was rejected by the Supreme Court without meaningful explanation.[41]

The principle of judicial restraint may account for the Court's different stance in Title VII and constitutional disparate impact cases. Consider these arguments that the intent requirement reflects a distinctively white manner of thinking about race discrimination: First, white people tend to view intent as an essential element of racial harm; nonwhites do not. The white perspective can be, and frequently is, expressed succinctly and without any apparent perceived need for justification: "[W]ithout concern about past and present intent, racially discriminatory effects of legislation would be quite innocent."[42] For black people, however, the fact of racial oppression exists largely independent of the motives or intentions of its perpetrators.[43] Second, both in principle and in application, the *Davis* rule presupposes the existence of race-neutral decisionmaking. Whites' level of confidence in race neutrality is much greater than nonwhites'; a skeptic (nonwhite, more likely than not) would not adopt a rule that presumes the neutrality of criteria of decision absent the specific intent to do racial harm. Finally, retaining the intent requirement in the face of its demonstrated failure to effectuate substantive racial justice is indicative of a complacency concerning, or even a commitment to, the racial status quo that can only be enjoyed by those who are its beneficiaries— by white people.[44] Thus the requirement of discriminatory intent represents the dominant, and in that sense traditional, way of thinking about race discrimination.

A Court responsive to the judicial restraint principle would be more hesitant to depart from this dominant understanding of discrimination when interpreting the Constitution than when interpreting a statute, because in the latter instance majoritarian correction would be more readily available. Thus, though the Court apparently did diverge from the prevailing intent-based conception of race discrimination when interpreting Title VII in *Griggs,* the explanation for its different position when confronted with a constitutional case, not found in *Davis,* may be institutional. Indeed, the *Davis* opinion contains a suggestion of this consideration: "[I]n our view, extension of the rule beyond those areas where it is already applicable by reason of statute, such as in the field of public employment, should await legislative prescription."[45] In this way, then, concern over the legitimacy of judicial review seems to have played a role in tailoring the substantive contours of Equal Protection doctrine to conform to what is "traditional" in our society.

A second effect of the pervasive principle of judicial restraint is the Court's concern with the "bottom-line" implications of particular doctrines. In *Washington v. Davis* the Court reasoned:

A rule that a statute designed to serve neutral ends is nevertheless invalid, absent compelling justification, if in practice it benefits or burdens one race more than another would be far reaching and would raise serious questions about, and perhaps invalidate, a whole range of tax, welfare, public service, regulatory, and licensing statutes that may be more burdensome to the poor and to the average black than to the more affluent white.[46]

One reading of this passage understands it to assert that applying strict scrutiny in all disparate impact cases would engage the courts too extensively in overseeing social policy.

Such activity arguably would be institutionally inappropriate solely by virtue of the volume of decisions involved; it is not seemly for the Court to appear to have a hand in managing such a wide range of policy choices. From the perspective of judicial restraint, an "effects test" would contravene the principle favoring limited use of the power of judicial review.

Another interpretation of the above passage illustrates the third way in which the principle of judicial restraint has affected race discrimination law. On this reading, the quoted language expresses a concern that a disparate impact approach might require the courts to engage in a form of economic redistribution. This concern partially dovetails with the first: Because economic redistribution is not a widely shared value, courts sensitive to issues of institutional legitimacy are doubly wary of adopting a doctrine that seemingly has such redistributive effects.

Though the principle of judicial restraint explains the Court's adoption of the requirement of discriminatory intent, it does not in the final analysis constitute a compelling argument against abandoning that requirement, as does, for example, the proposed transparency-conscious constitutional rule. First, the problem of legitimacy is less pressing when judicial review is predicated on an explicit constitutional text, such as the Equal Protection Clause.[47] Accordingly, one might have thought that race discrimination doctrine would be relatively insulated from the concern over the legitimacy of judicial review. One explanation for the degree to which the latter does exert an influence is that focusing on problems of judicial role deflects discussion of the difficult substantive issue discussed in the preceding section: whether the guarantee of equal protection embodies a colorblindness or antisubordinative principle.[48] However, discomfort with the task of engaging in a candid consideration of constitutional values is no justification for not doing so.

Perhaps, then, the most pressing implication of the principle of judicial restraint is the final one: A disparate impact approach might require courts to engage in a form of economic redistribution. Of course, the proposed transparency-conscious rule would not cut so deeply into the economic status quo as would the alternative rejected by the *Davis* Court: strict scrutiny of all rules with racially disparate effects. Because the proposed rule imposes a lower level of scrutiny on a finding of disproportionate impact, government's burden of justification would be more easily sustained, and thus there would be fewer instances of judicial invalidation with which to be concerned.

Nevertheless, the proposed rule does have, and is intended to have, some racially redistributive effects. The *Davis* argument points out a core dilemma in liberal egalitarian rhetoric: While we approve and are willing in some respects to foster racial equality, we endorse no similar economic egalitarianism. Indeed, the mainstream view in this society seems to be that "equal stratification"—a proportionate representation of nonwhites at each economic level—would achieve racial equality.[49] Thus, because our history of the overt and covert, intentional and thoughtless oppression of blacks by whites has placed the former in a relatively disadvantaged economic position, any attempt at racial reform runs afoul of our at least equally strong resistance to intervention in the existing distribution of economic goods, a resistance that is especially acute when the federal judiciary assumes responsibility to alter the status quo.

The solution to the dilemma, I think, is for white people to acknowledge that taking responsibility for race discrimination does and should cost something.[50] Implementing "Test 22" will indeed mean that fewer white officers will be hired onto the D.C. police force; employing criteria of selection that place more blacks in policymaking positions may well mean that government expends funds differently than before and expends relatively less to benefit whites. If the status quo results from a long history of the systematic privileging of whites, as it surely does, then one can only expect that a more racially just society would see a different, and more equal, distribution of societal goods.

The proposed rule in fact has relatively modest redistributive effects. It does no more than require government not to pursue thoughtlessly goals that advantage whites, and it permits nonwhites to propose inclusive means of accomplishing permissible goals; it does not mandate absolute distributional equality. It lays some of the burden of formulating more inclusive strategies at the feet of nonwhites, but it requires government to adopt those strategies whenever possible. To that extent, the proposed rule mandates a modest transfer of power as well as a somewhat more racially just distribution of benefits and burdens. We whites should expect no less from any rule that attempts seriously to address the structural racism of which transparency is one manifestation.

[5]

Disparate Impact under Title VII

TITLE VII OF the Civil Rights Act of 1964 governs discrimination in employment, and currently includes a doctrine that predicates liability upon proof of disparate impact alone, without requiring the plaintiff to establish discriminatory intent. Even in the absence of that requirement, however, existing Title VII doctrine requires modification if it is to provide a remedy for transparently white decisionmaking. After exploring the deficiencies in the current rules, this chapter proposes two transparency-conscious alternatives, paying special attention to the fact that Title VII, unlike the Constitution, regulates private conduct.

Two Hypothetical Cases

Goodson, Badwin & Indiff is a major accounting firm employing more than five hundred persons nationwide. Among its twenty black accountants is Yvonne Taylor, who at the time this story begins was thirty-one years old and poised to become the first black regional supervisor in the firm's history. Yvonne attended Princeton University and received an M.B.A. from the Kellogg Graduate School of Management at Northwestern University. While employed at Goodson, she was very successful in attracting new clients, especially from the black business community. In all other respects her performance at the firm was regarded as exemplary as well.

Yvonne always was comfortable conforming to the norms of the corporate culture at Goodson, and in fact has been comfortable with "white" norms since childhood. Her manner of speech, dress, and hairstyle, as well as many of her attitudes and beliefs, fall well within the bounds of whites' cultural expectations. However, Yvonne may have adapted to the corporate culture too well. It is common practice at Goodson to be less than absolutely precise in keeping records of one's billable hours. Instead, accountants generally estimate time spent on clients' accounts at the end of each day, and tend to err on the side of over- rather than underbilling. On the rare occasions this practice is discussed, it is explained in terms of the firm's prestige in the business community; the subtext is that clients should consider themselves fortunate to be associated with Goodson at all. Like other young accountants, Yvonne at first attempted to keep meticulous records, but she soon realized that others were surpassing her in billable hours without spending more time actually at work. Consequently, and consistent with her general pattern of conforming to prevailing norms, she gradually adopted the less precise method.

Under Goodson's promotion procedure, the decision

whether to promote an accountant to regional supervisor rests on senior partners' evaluations of the candidate's accounting knowledge and skills and, to a lesser extent, on assessments of her interpersonal skills solicited from clients and from peers in the office in which she works. The reports on Yvonne's accounting skills were uniformly excellent. Comments from some peers had overtones of distance and mild distrust suggesting that they were somewhat uncomfortable with Yvonne as a black woman, but these comments fell far below the level necessary to raise serious doubts about her interpersonal skills. However, several of Yvonne's clients took the occasion to register complaints about possible overbilling. The firm launched an extensive investigation and eventually reached the conclusion that Yvonne had been careless in her recordkeeping and that therefore she should not be promoted at that time. As a practical matter, this episode ended Yvonne's prospects for advancement at Goodson; the firm has an informal policy of not reconsidering an individual once she has been passed over for promotion.

Yvonne has a younger sister who, sometime during college, legally changed her name from Deborah Taylor to Keisha Akbar. As her decision to change her name suggests, Keisha places an emphasis on her African heritage that Yvonne does not, and she has adopted speech and grooming patterns consistent with that cultural perspective. For example, Keisha often wears clothing that features African styles and materials, frequently braids her hair or wears it in a natural style, and at times speaks to other black employees in "Black English," though she always uses "standard English" when speaking with whites. Keisha majored in biology at

Howard University, and after graduation went to work as the only black scientist at a small research firm dedicated to identifying and developing environmentally safe agricultural products for commercial uses. Like Yvonne, Keisha excelled at the technical aspects of her work, but she brought to it a much less assimilationist personal style. At first, her cultural differences had no particular impact on her job performance. This changed, however, when the once-small firm began to grow rapidly and reorganization into research divisions became necessary. For the most part, the firm planned to elevate each of the original members of the research team to positions as department heads, but Keisha was not asked to head a department because the individuals responsible for making that decision felt that she lacked the personal qualities that a successful manager needs. They saw Keisha as just too different from the researchers she would supervise to be able to communicate effectively with them. The firm articulated this reasoning by asserting a need for a department head who shared the perspectives and values of the employees under her direction. When Keisha raised the possibility that her perceived differences might be race-dependent, the decisionmakers replied that they would apply the same conformity-related criteria to white candidates for the position of department head.

Thus, in spite of the diametrically different cultural styles adopted by Yvonne and Keisha,[1] their stories have the same ending: Each encountered the glass ceiling at a relatively early stage of what should have been a very successful career.[2] A case can be made that both were disadvantaged because of race. Yvonne would argue that there is no nonracial element of her performance or her personal characteristics that could account for the way her recordkeeping practices were singled out for special scrutiny, and therefore that race is left as the most plausible explanation of the different treatment she received. Even if the basis for the special treatment was unconscious, this is a relatively easily understood form of discrimination: Yvonne's contention would be that she was treated differently from similarly situated colleagues because of her race.

Keisha, on the other hand, arguably was given the same treatment that would have been afforded anyone who was perceived as unable or unwilling to fit smoothly into the corporate culture. Nevertheless, it can be argued that she too was disadvantaged because of her race, in that the personal characteristics that disqualified her from a management position intersect seamlessly with her self-definition as a black woman. In effect, she was subjected to transparently white decisionmaking; Keisha would argue that she was not promoted because her personal style was found wanting when measured against a norm that was in fact transparently "white."

Because these race-specific acts occurred in employment contexts, both Yvonne and Keisha would turn to Title VII for legal relief. However, even though Title VII provides a cause of action for adverse employment decisions taken "because of" race,[3] Keisha and Yvonne would find themselves in quite different positions under existing judicial interpretations of that statute. Yvonne would have a relatively easy time framing a disparate treatment claim (though that is not to say that she necessarily would prevail), but as a practical matter Keisha would have difficulty getting beyond the initial pleading stage because the form of discrimination she encountered cannot easily be addressed under either the disparate treatment or the current disparate impact model. After describing these two approaches to Title VII liability, I will examine the strengths and weaknesses of two alternatives that would provide a remedy for transparently white decisionmaking.

Existing Models of Title VII Liability

The rule governing Title VII disparate treatment cases initially was set forth in *McDonnell Douglas Corp. v. Green.*[4] The plaintiff must establish a prima facie case of discrimination, which may be made

by showing (i) that he belongs to a racial minority; (ii) that he applied and was qualified for a job for which the employer was seeking applicants; (iii) that, despite his qualifications, he was rejected; and (iv) that, after his rejection, the position remained open and the employer continued to seek applicants from persons of complainant's qualifications.[5]

The elements of the prima facie case may be modified to suit employment settings that differ from the facts of *McDonnell Douglas.*

The burden then shifts to the defendant to articulate a legitimate, nondiscriminatory explanation for the adverse employment action. This is only a burden of production, and not of proof; the burden of persuasion remains at all times with the plaintiff.[6] If such an explanation is advanced by the defendant, the plaintiff must prove that the proffered reason was not the real reason for the challenged action. The plaintiff must demonstrate not only that the articulated reason is not credible, but that it is a pretext for discrimination. That is, the plaintiff must not only disprove the employer's legitimate, nondiscriminatory explanation, but also must show that race was the real reason for the adverse action.[7]

If Yvonne wished to pursue a Title VII claim, she would frame it as a case of disparate treatment, arguing that similarly situated white accountants who followed the same practice of imprecise recordkeeping were not denied promotions because of it. This would be a question of fact that would turn on evidentiary issues beyond the scope of this discussion. The significance of Yvonne's case for present purposes is that it fits easily within the conceptual framework of existing Title VII case law, and so she would have at least the opportunity to reach the factual question whether she was treated differently from similarly situated white accountants.[8]

Keisha's complaint is conceptually distinct from a disparate treatment claim, which centers on the notion that the employer treated the plaintiff differently from similarly situated others. In contrast to Yvonne's claim, Keisha would argue that though she was treated in the same manner as others, the standard applied to all employees is one that systematically advantages whites. One might suppose, then, that her claim might be framed under the disparate impact theory of liability. However, a careful review of the requirements of a disparate impact claim reveals that Keisha would not fare well under that approach, either.

In a Title VII disparate impact case, the plaintiff's prima

facie case requires a showing that a facially neutral employment practice has a disproportionately adverse impact on a
protected class. Once that threshold is reached, the burden of
persuasion shifts to the employer to demonstrate that the
challenged practice is job-related and justifiable as a matter
of business necessity. Finally, the plaintiff has an opportunity
to prove that there exists an alternative practice that would
serve the employer's objectives equally well but have a less
severe adverse effect.[9]

The disparate impact approach to Title VII liability has
been deeply affected by the Civil Rights Act of 1991.[10] First,
the Act finally placed disparate impact analysis on a secure
statutory foundation.[11] Second, Congress overruled some aspects of *Wards Cove Packing Co. v. Atonio,*[12] a 1989 case
that provided a good part of the motivation for the 1991
Act. In *Wards Cove,* the Supreme Court had announced a
series of changes in disparate impact doctrine. Most notable
among these pronouncements were a new rule that the issue
of business necessity was not to be seen as an affirmative
defense, but rather as part of the plaintiff's case, and a re-
definition of the concept of business necessity to become
more a notion of reasonable justification than of *necessity.*[13]
In the 1991 Act, Congress made it clear that the burden of
persuasion on the question of business necessity rests on
the employer, rather than the plaintiff.[14] Moreover, the Act
reinstated judicial interpretations of "consistent with business necessity" and "job relatedness" that predated *Wards
Cove.*

The first element of a disparate impact case is the requirement that the plaintiff prove that a particular employment

practice actually has an adverse impact on a protected group. The issues that may arise at this stage include the choice of comparison groups—e.g., general population versus qualified labor force[15]—the geographic region and time frame within which the comparison is made, the degree of disproportion between the compared groups, the accuracy of the relevant data, and the statistical methods employed to assess the significance of identified disparities.[16] One *Wards Cove* ruling left virtually untouched by the 1991 Act is the requirement that the plaintiff identify a particular employment practice (or inseparable cluster of practices) claimed to have caused the disparate effect.[17]

Once the plaintiff has established the existence of disparate effects, the burden of persuasion shifts to the defendant to show that the challenged practice is job-related and justified as a matter of business necessity. The nature of this burden remains somewhat unclear. In the case that first set forth the disparate impact approach, *Griggs v. Duke Power Co.*,[18] the Court said that the defendant must show that a challenged practice has "a demonstrable relationship to successful performance of the jobs for which it [is] used."[19] This rather vague formulation leaves unresolved a number of important questions regarding the business necessity justification: the kind of purposes that suffice as justification, the kind of proof necessary to establish a relationship between the purpose and the challenged practice, the requisite strength of that connection, the importance of the employer's asserted purpose, and the relationship between the concepts of business necessity and job relatedness.[20] None of these issues has been definitively resolved by the Supreme Court.

Finally, even if the defendant succeeds in establishing business necessity, the plaintiff may prevail by demonstrating the existence of an alternative selection criterion with no, or less severe, disparate effects, if the employer refuses to adopt the alternative practice.[21] It remains to be seen whether "refusing" to adopt an alternative criterion means only a failure to use it, or requires knowledge of its existence as well.

Disparate impact theory has undergone several changes during the past few years. The language in *Griggs v. Duke Power Co.* seemed to make it clear that discriminatory intent was not a necessary component of a Title VII disparate impact case.[22] However, the Court gradually moved toward the view that disparate impact was to be seen as nothing more than an indirect method of proving discriminatory intent. The Court began this drift in *Albemarle Paper Co. v. Moody,*[23] the first disparate impact case to reach the Court after *Griggs.* In *Albemarle,* the Court borrowed from the structure of disparate treatment analysis to establish a parallel framework for disparate impact cases. That is, under both theories there was to be a tripartite order of proof: The plaintiff would make out a prima facie case; the defendant would have an opportunity to provide a neutral explanation or justification; and the plaintiff would then attempt to discredit the neutral explanation or justification. This structural symmetry laid the foundation for deeper theoretical convergence.

In discussing the third stage of analysis—the plaintiff's opportunity for rebuttal—the Court in *Albemarle* employed language that strongly suggested an intent-based interpretation of disparate impact liability:

If an employer does then meet the burden of proving that its tests are "job related," it remains open to the complaining party to show that other tests or selection devices, without a similarly undesirable racial effect, would also serve the employer's legitimate interest in "efficient and trustworthy workmanship." Such a showing would be evidence that the employer was using its tests merely as a "pretext" for discrimination.[24]

Similar "pretext" language appears in two of the other three leading Supreme Court disparate impact decisions.[25] The implication, of course, is that the plaintiff's ultimate objective in a disparate impact claim is to demonstrate that the defendant intentionally employed a facially neutral criterion of decision *because of* its discriminatory effects.[26]

This implication was strengthened by another post-*Griggs* change in the Court's position. For several years after *Griggs,* the Court seemed to adhere to the view that the defendant bears the burden of persuasion on the question of business necessity. However, in *Watson v. Fort Worth Bank & Trust*[27] a plurality of the Justices suggested that the burden of persuasion on this issue ought to rest with the plaintiff,[28] and in *Wards Cove* a majority of the Court took this position.[29] As Justice Stevens explained in dissent, the Court's former view that business necessity is an affirmative defense—with the burden of persuasion falling on the defendant—presupposes an understanding that disparate impact liability is not linked to motive or intent.[30] By implication, then, placing the burden of persuasion on the plaintiff signals rejection of that conception of disparate impact liability and indirectly confirms the view that disparate impact is no more than an indirect means of establishing discriminatory intent. However, in the Civil Rights Act of 1991, Congress reallocated the burden of persuasion to the defendant on the issue of business necessity, and in so doing made it clear that the disparate impact theory of liability is not tied to the notion of discriminatory intent.

It should be apparent that Yvonne has no disparate impact claim; the essence of her complaint is that she was treated differently from other, similarly situated accountants. One might suppose, however, that Keisha would be able to pursue a Title VII claim under the disparate impact theory of liability, contending that she was disadvantaged by the use of a facially neutral criterion of decision that inevitably will have an adverse effect on blacks as a group. This supposition might be correct in theory, but it would not be borne out in practice. Keisha would encounter several technical barriers that would, in practical effect, foreclose her claim.

First, the disparate impact plaintiff must have statistically significant evidence of racial imbalance in the workforce. In addition to the usual problems of choosing appropriate bases for comparison, Keisha's ability to make out a prima facie case would be impeded by the relatively small size of the workforce at her place of employment and the even smaller number of black persons employed there. Inferences based on small samples can be misleading because they may suggest short-term results that will not hold true over a longer period; or, to put it somewhat differently, the effect of a particular employment practice on two individuals may not look the same as the effect of that practice on two hundred persons. Courts, therefore, often are reluctant to accept statistical proof based on small samples.[31] The small sample size problem may be exacerbated by the EEOC's "four-fifths" rule, which states that a selection rate for members of a protected group that is less than 80 percent of the selection rate for the most successful group will be deemed evidence of an adverse impact.[32] Such a rule, of course, is highly unreliable as applied to small samples.[33]

Keisha might have been employed at a company large enough to provide a basis for the requisite statistical comparisons and so might evade the problem of small sample size. But even under these circumstances, she might confront a second hurdle, a variant of the "bottom-line problem," if the company employed an adequate number of "Yvonnes" to counter her claim that blacks were underrepresented in the relevant employee pool. While this issue ought to be considered resolved by the Court's reasoning in *Connecticut v. Teal*,[34] Keisha's case requires application to a new context. *Teal* asked whether an employer could justify its use of a criterion that adversely impacted a racial group by pointing to the absence of disparate effects at the "bottom line"; the defendant argued that use of a criterion that overselected blacks at a later stage of a decisionmaking process should defeat a challenge to the use of a criterion that underselected blacks at an earlier stage, if the bottom-line results showed no racial disparity. The Court rejected this line of argument, elevating the procedural rights of the individual over the group interest in ultimate outcomes. By analogy, Keisha's individual right not to be disadvantaged by an unjustified criterion of decision that negatively affects black persons like her should not be undercut by the fact that the same criterion would not have a similar impact on people like Yvonne.

A third hurdle Keisha would have to surmount is some courts' indecision over the question whether the plaintiff must prove the existence of a disparate impact in the employer's workforce. In *EEOC v. Greyhound Lines, Inc.*,[35] the Third Circuit held that workforce statistics are a necessary element of a disparate impact claim.[36] However, in *Dothard v. Rawlinson*[37] the Supreme Court appeared to accept proof of a disparate effect in the form of national statistics on the average height and weight of men and women; the Court did not require a showing that the employer's height and weight requirements had a negative impact on the representation of women in the employer's own workforce.[38] I believe the Court's view in *Dothard* is the correct one even under existing disparate impact analysis, with respect to immutable characteristics that one can expect to be evenly distributed in the general population, such as height and weight. However, in the case of characteristics that are perceived to be mutable and that are not evenly distributed, one has to acknowledge that there is some force to the argument that abandoning the workplace requirement could unfairly impose liability on an employer whose practices had not in fact created a racially imbalanced workforce. Grooming standards would provide an example: Suppose that an employer prohibited the wearing of "dredlocks," and suppose that it could be established that such a requirement would have a negative impact on the class of black employees generally. It would not follow that the employer's prohibition actually had a negative impact in his workplace, and so imposing liability for what merely might happen could be said to be unjust. Thus the workforce requirement cannot be dismissed lightly.

Once the plaintiff establishes the existence of a racially disproportionate distribution, she must prove causation; that is, she must identify a specific employment practice (or inseparable group of practices) responsible for the identified disparity and demonstrate a causal connection between the two. Here, the subjective nature of the decision makes it unlikely that the transparency plaintiff will be able to identify the precise reasons for the adverse decision in her case, or to document the criteria employed in other cases in which candidates for promotion were successful.[39] Moreover, because of the inherent indeterminacy of subjective criteria, even if the plaintiff can *name* the criteria actually employed, she will have an extremely difficult time showing that those criteria *caused* the disparate impact in question.

A second aspect of the causation issue is the problem of choice. Courts have frequently taken the view that a particular employment practice cannot be said to have a racially disproportionate effect if the disadvantaged employees could have chosen to conform their conduct to the employer's requirements.[40] The clearest instances of this reasoning can be found in the grooming and language cases. In *Rogers v. American Airlines*,[41] a black woman plaintiff whose hair was styled in "cornrows" challenged a prohibition against wearing braided hair on the job. The court refused to credit the policy's disproportionately negative impact on black women employees, and also expressed the view that the employer should not be held liable for the allegedly discriminatory decision because it resulted from the employee's own grooming choice. For similar reasons, most cases considering English-only workplace rules have come down in favor of the

employer.[42] Keisha's case might fall prey to the same ratio-
nale, as one can argue that the existence of women like
Yvonne illuminates the contingent nature of the personal
choices Keisha has made.

None of these barriers is absolute; for each, it can be
argued that a plaintiff like Keisha should be able to set forth
a prima facie case under existing disparate impact analysis.
Nevertheless, the cumulative effect of these obstacles is significant. With respect to each of them except the documentation problem, courts may rule that Keisha cannot prevail
regardless of the strength of the evidence she can produce.
Since the plaintiff bears the burden of persuasion on each of
these points, the likelihood that she will be able to establish
a prima facie case diminishes exponentially with each addition to the list of problematic points of law.

It is important to recognize that these technical difficulties
are not random or accidental; they are linked to the nature
of Keisha's claim. Transparently white decisionmaking consists of the unconscious use of criteria of decision that are
more strongly associated with whites than with nonwhites.
This phenomenon is most likely to occur in settings where
nonwhites are tokens; that is, where they represent a very
small percentage of the workforce.[43] In a more diversified
environment (assuming one that is not racially stratified), it
is much more likely that criteria of decision are conscious
and perhaps contested. The small sample size and workforce
problems are likely to occur in those same settings in which
transparently white decisionmaking is most likely to take
place—that is, workplaces with very few nonwhites. In addition, the transparency phenomenon under consideration here
involves subjective criteria of decision, which always raise

the problems of documentation and choice. Thus, while these problems occur in a broader category of cases than those implicating transparency, they are inevitably present in any transparency case with which this discussion is concerned.

Because the imposition of transparently white norms amounts to a requirement that nonwhite employees assimilate to whites' cultural expectations, another way to frame the fundamental issue raised by Keisha's case is to ask whether there ought to be a Title VII remedy for an employer's failure to create a culturally pluralistic workplace. Attention to the transparency phenomenon and the circumstances in which it is most likely to occur should guide formulation of an alternative conceptual framework in which Keisha would have a reasonable chance to succeed in a Title VII claim.

Two New Models of Liability

Each of the two models presented here implements Title VII's proscription of employment decisions taken "because of" race more effectively than the existing disparate impact model, as applied to transparently white decisionmaking. The foreseeable impact model parallels the structure of current disparate impact analysis, but substitutes proof of foreseeable effects for the current requirement that the plaintiff establish the existence of an actual disparate effect. The second model, labeled the alternatives approach, takes the structural context of employer decisionmaking as its point of departure.

The Foreseeable Impact Model

The foreseeable impact model tracks traditional disparate impact analysis, but institutes modifications at appropriate points in the analytic structure in order to accommodate the unique features of Keisha's transparency claim. In particular, this approach adopts a new method of establishing the existence of a disparate effect and emphasizes the problem of assimilationism through its analyses of the employer's business necessity defense and the plaintiff's presentation of less discriminatory alternatives.

The first stage of a disparate impact case is the plaintiff's proof that an identified criterion of decision (or set of criteria, if the components are inseparable)[44] had a statistically significant differential impact on the racial composition of the workforce at her place of employment. As described above, under existing disparate impact analysis Keisha would encounter (at least) five distinct difficulties in setting forth her prima facie case. In combination, these doctrinal hurdles present a formidable obstacle to the success of any transparency claim. Current doctrine's focus on actual effects can render it a very effective tool for addressing many forms of discrimination.[45] However, Keisha's case calls for an emphasis on foreseeable, rather than actual, disproportionate effects. The essence of her claim is that the application of culturally white norms necessarily operates to the disadvantage of nonwhites, given the existing social construction of race and concomitant racial hierarchy. One has only to understand the racial structure of American society to be able to conclude that employing criteria of decision formulated against the background of white paradigms will have an inevitable and negative impact on the employment prospects of nonwhites as a group.

The next question, then, is how one might structure proof of foreseeable disparate effects. From the perspective of the transparency phenomenon, the problem in Keisha's case is the application of norms whose content is in some sense white-specific; it follows that conformity to those norms is inherently more problematic for her than for a white person. The difficulty, of course, is to distinguish facially neutral criteria of decision that are in fact white-specific from those that are genuinely race-neutral.[46] In outline, the factors that differentiate a white-specific criterion are (1) that the criterion be associated with whites to a greater extent than with nonwhites, and (2) that it be favorably regarded by whites.[47] More generally, it is the *norm underlying* a judgment that must be associated with whites and positively regarded; in some instances the label actually ascribed to the individual who is being evaluated carries negative import, as when Delores (the Board candidate in chapter 1) was characterized as "hostile."

The first requirement, that a facially neutral criterion be associated more closely with whites than with other racial groups if it is to be considered white-specific, is a broad requirement that implicates a wide range of characteristics that might be distributed unevenly across races. It includes criteria that are biological in origin (for example, blond hair and blue eyes), but extends equally to characteristics that are associated with whites as a consequence of the existing social hierarchy of race, as well as to differences that are more purely cultural in origin. The requirement is easily satisfied; one need only show that the criterion of decision in question is one that occurs more frequently among whites than among other racial groups.

The second requirement, that the criterion at issue be one that is favorably regarded by whites, is directed more toward the transparency thesis than toward the notion of white specificity per se. Because transparency analysis targets the unconscious use of white-specific criteria to disadvantage nonwhites, it would not make sense to be concerned with characteristics that are associated with white people but viewed negatively.[48] The same consideration applies to the foreseeable impact analysis under development here, because the plaintiff in a foreseeable impact case would of course be required to show a *negative* impact on nonwhites.

Thus the first stage of a foreseeable impact claim would require the plaintiff to demonstrate only that an unfavorable employment decision was based on lack of a characteristic more frequently possessed by whites than by nonwhites;[49] it would follow without further proof that use of that criterion would have a negative impact on the employment prospects of nonwhites as a group. Keisha, then, would only have to show that her employer's conformity requirement implicitly incorporated characteristics more often found in whites than in nonwhites. This approach to disparate impact cases would circumvent most of the difficulties described earlier. It would avoid all of the problems associated with the current requirement that a disparate impact plaintiff prove actual disparate effects (that is, the problems of small sample size, bottom-line impact, and workforce statistics). In addition, it would mitigate the problems of causation and choice. Though the issue of documentation would remain, a plaintiff in Keisha's position would be able to proceed solely on the basis of the criterion offered by her employer to explain the adverse action taken against her; she would not have to make comparisons either with actual decisions or with the criteria applied to other employees. Similarly, the problem of choice would be diminished. A showing that nonwhites as a group are less likely than whites to possess the desired characteristic would tend to divert attention from the individual to the differential distribution itself. That is, the assumption that the plaintiff's personal attributes are a product of individual choice could be supplanted, at least in part, by attention to the societal structures that constrain and condition individual will.[50]

The foreseeable impact framework would retain business necessity as an affirmative defense, and thus would place the burden of persuasion on the employer to show job relatedness and business necessity.[51] Because the focus here is the problem of assimilationism, this defense should be interpreted narrowly to exclude justifications that reproduce assimilation in another form. In Keisha's case, for example, the employer should not be able to prevail on the basis of an argument that a homogeneous workforce is inherently a more productive one. On the other hand, this proposal does not rule out assimilationist defenses altogether. This discussion focuses on the application of Title VII to private employers (though it applies to government employers as well), and I do not assume that such employers have an absolute obligation to pursue pluralist objectives or to employ pluralist means of attaining permissible goals. Thus this situation differs from the constitutional context, because I believe that government does have a general obligation to proceed in a pluralist manner. Consequently the burden on private employers ought to be somewhat lighter than that placed on government in chapter 3. Even so, the boundary between what constitutes permissible assimilationism in the Title VII context and what does not is difficult to define in the abstract. A good starting point might be the proposition that an employer may require assimilation only when necessary to preserve the essence of the business.[52]

A foreseeable impact analysis would raise issues not implicated by the current actual impact approach. Some of these would be familiar, in the sense that similar questions arise in other legal contexts. For example, the foreseeable impact plaintiff would be required to show that the characteristic, or norm, that is the basis for an adverse decision is white-specific in the sense described above; she would have to introduce admissible evidence of differential distribution on a society-wide basis.[53] That would almost certainly require sociological evidence, which would raise the evidentiary issues generally presented by the introduction of expert testimony.

Some of the issues presented by the foreseeable impact framework, however, would be unique to this analysis. For example, a defendant might challenge the plaintiff's claim of differential distribution on the basis of race by introducing evidence of a differential distribution among subgroups of nonwhites, accompanied by a showing that the characteristic in question occurs in the plaintiff's subgroup with approximately the same frequency it does among whites. In turn, this argument would, or ought to, raise the question whether the subgroupings chosen by the defendant exist because of assimilationist pressures. When that is the case, the subgrouping approach ought to be disapproved as a means of defending against the plaintiff's proof of society-wide differential distribution because it functions to reinstate assimilationism.

Thus, Keisha's employers might argue that their "conformity" requirement would not disadvantage black scientists, even though it would have a differential impact on the black population generally. They would claim that black people who are trained as scientists are as likely as whites to possess the cultural characteristics they seek. However, this argument simply overlooks the assimilationist pressures on blacks who choose to enter scientific (and other professional) fields. Thus this sort of defense ought not to succeed.

In spite of these novel difficulties, one might conclude that the issues presented by a foreseeable impact approach, formidable as they appear at first, are in reality no less manageable than the statistical issues that have to be resolved under current actual impact doctrine. Surely the courts' demonstrated ability to negotiate the hypertechnical terrain of statistical proof counsels that one ought not reject prematurely the possibility of developing a workable framework for foreseeable impact cases.

However, there is a deeper flaw in the foreseeable impact approach, one that is not as amenable to practical resolution as the technical matters just described may be. This difficulty lies in the fact that the foreseeable impact model posits differences between whites as a group and nonwhites as a group.

Even if the proposition that there are such racial differences turns out to be descriptively accurate with respect to one or more challenged criteria of decision, relying on this difference model as the foundation for legal analysis may be normatively problematic in two respects. For some, the ascription of racial difference would be inconsistent with the norm of colorblindness. From this perspective, it would be undesirable, and perhaps necessarily unworkable, to anchor a legal doctrine on a premise so at odds with the fundamental, if aspirational, values of society. For others, the ascription of difference might not be troubling in itself, but predictable social processes virtually would assure that attributes associated with whites would be seen as the norm, and that attributes associated with nonwhites would be perceived as deviant.[54] For these critics, this aspect of the foreseeable impact approach comes too close to a connotation of inherent inferiority to be normatively acceptable.

I believe that these disturbing normative implications arise because the foreseeable impact approach treats white specificity as an issue of fact, in the sense that a particular criterion of decision either is white-specific, or it is not; in turn, that question depends on the existence *vel non* of some "real difference" between racial groups. I think, however, that it is much more accurate a description of social dynamics to characterize a conclusion regarding white specificity as contextual and therefore contingent. That is, it is not the criterion in the abstract that is white-specific, but the criterion in the context of its usage. This insight suggests another statutory avenue for implementing liability for transparently white decisionmaking—one that focuses on context rather than content.

The Alternatives Model

This model departs from the existing disparate impact framework in favor of an approach that more directly captures the structural nature of the discrimination Keisha experienced. In outline, analysis of a nonwhite plaintiff's claim regarding an adverse employment decision would proceed as follows. The plaintiff's first step would be to analyze the racial structure of her workplace.[55] A showing that the plaintiff's place of employment is predominantly white, or structured in such a way that whites predominate in positions of authority, would trigger a presumption that the adverse action rested on white-specific criteria of decision. However, that showing alone would not shift the burden of persuasion to the defendant. The employer would have to articulate the criterion employed in reaching the challenged decision, and the objectives served by it, but the plaintiff would bear the burden of proposing an alternative criterion that would serve the employer's objective equally well, and in a manner satisfactory to the plaintiff. Finally, the defendant would have an opportunity to persuade the court that adopting the proposed alternative would require unreasonable measures.

Like the foreseeable impact approach, the alternatives model is grounded in the disparate impact provision of the Civil Rights Act of 1991. That provision is structured in this way: A disparate impact violation is established only if (i) the plaintiff demonstrates the existence of a disparate impact and the employer fails to demonstrate job relatedness and business necessity; or (ii) the plaintiff demonstrates the existence of an alternative practice and the employer refuses to adopt it.[56] There are three possible interpretations of this structure.

Upon plaintiff's demonstration of disparate impact, interpretation (A) understands the plaintiff's proof of less discriminatory alternatives to come into play only if the defendant establishes business necessity, while interpretation (B) permits the plaintiff to move directly from impact to consideration of alternatives, and thus to circumvent the business necessity stage.[57] Finally, interpretation (C) sees the Act as stating that proof of a disparate impact is not necessary when the plaintiff can demonstrate the availability of an alternative practice. Of course, interpretation (C) follows the structure of the statutory language. However, the 1991 Act also adopts pre–*Wards Cove* precedents in regard to the meaning of "alternative employment practice." Because those precedents all involve cases in which the existence of a disparate impact was regarded as a prerequisite for consideration of the alternatives issue, it must be concluded that the 1991 Act did not intend to create structure (C).

The alternatives approach follows interpretation (B), and wholly discards the question of business necessity, substituting an inquiry into the existence of less assimilationist alternatives to a challenged business practice. Moreover, this approach infers the existence of a disparate impact from the confluence of two lines of reasoning. First, there is a structural analysis: Norms formulated in a dominantly white workplace are presumed to be white-specific and thus to have an adverse effect on nonwhites. Second, this model requires the plaintiff to formulate an alternative that will not disadvantage nonwhites at all, or one that will not disadvantage them as severely as the employer's challenged practice. The plaintiff will be able to do so only if the challenged criterion has some disparate effect. Thus, under the alternatives model disparate impact is not abandoned, but inferred.

The alternatives model mirrors the institutional nature of some forms of race discrimination. Keisha's claim, for example, is structural in the sense that it is the consequence of a particular workforce composition and the nature of white race consciousness. Therefore, it seems only natural to construct a doctrinal framework that reflects the structural character of this theory of liability, and thus disavow the intent-like connotations of the existing disparate impact approach. The alternatives model permits the plaintiff who has been disadvantaged by institutionally race-specific features of the workplace to rely on general knowledge about this form of race specificity, and to proceed directly to the exploration of more inclusive employment practices.

The first issue to be addressed under the alternatives model is whether the nonwhite plaintiff's workplace is predominantly white. Such workplaces fall into three categories. First, any circumstance in which nonwhites constitute less than roughly fifteen percent of the workforce should qualify for this characterization.[58] In addition, any workplace that is racially stratified, with whites occupying all or nearly all of the upper-level positions, should be considered a predominantly white workplace. Finally, there may be some instances in which a significant percentage of ostensibly managerial positions are occupied by nonwhites, but in which whites wield most or all of the ultimate policymaking authority; these too should be identified as predominantly white workplaces.

The second component of the alternatives model is the

plaintiff's obligation to formulate more racially inclusive means of accomplishing the employer's stated objectives. Of course, there must be some constraints on the range of permissible objectives, or the approach will have no impact at all on assimilationist employment practices. The scope of permissible objectives should be broad enough to include legitimate financial motives, but narrow enough to exclude matters of taste that are unnecessary for the attainment of those financial goals.[59] Moreover, the preferences of customers and clients that implicate the categories protected by Title VII should not be invoked at this stage, even if those preferences indirectly affect financial outcomes.[60]

Finally, at the heart of the alternatives model lies the question of what sort of alternatives the transparency plaintiff might put forward. Because the focus of this model is institutional discrimination, the range of alternatives available to the plaintiff should not be limited to alternative criteria of decision and, of course, the nature of an appropriate alternative will be highly case-specific. In Keisha's case, the problem is a white-specific vision of the characteristics needed in a scientific department head. In this sort of case, diversity training for white employees who are to be under Keisha's supervision, combined with clear indications of the firm's support for her, may be enough to solve the problem from her perspective.[61] To reduce the problem of white specificity in the future, the company also might provide diversity training for the individuals who were the decisionmakers in Keisha's case. In other cases, more drastic measures, such as restructuring chains of command, or reallocating decisionmaking authority, might be in order.

Under the alternatives model, the employer could defend by arguing that adopting a proposed alternative would not be reasonable. Thus the alternatives model would resolve the ultimate question of the extent to which an assimilationist workplace is permissible under an analysis very similar to established concepts of reasonable accommodation, rather than business necessity. As with the foreseeable impact model, however, the line in question is very difficult to draw in the abstract.

Like the foreseeable impact approach, the alternatives framework implicates some concepts that are relatively unfamiliar in legal analysis. Indeed, the approach is founded on the unusual proposition that norms developed in predominantly white settings are presumptively white-specific. On the other hand, the alternatives model presents fewer technical problems than the foreseeable impact framework. Moreover, on one level it is less normatively problematic. It represents a direct, structural response to a structural problem, and adheres to the skepticism preferred by transparency theory. Thus, if one accepts the premises of the transparency analyses presented in chapters 1 and 2, the alternatives approach would appear to be the most fitting doctrinal framework for implementing a remedy.

The weakness of the alternatives model lies in its substitution of skepticism for a fact-oriented approach to the question of disparate effects. For those inclined to regard the question of white specificity as a resolvable question of fact, the alternatives approach may seem overinclusive. It threatens to impose liability, through the presumption of race specificity, on employers whose criteria of decision are not in fact race-specific. This result seems inconsistent with the notion that Title VII aims to preserve a realm of autonomy for private employers.

Comparing the Foreseeable Impact and Alternatives Models

The approaches examined here differ in two respects. First, they diverge with regard to the way "disparate impact"—the employer's use of white-specific criteria—may be established. The foreseeable impact model focuses on the content of challenged criteria of decision and treats the existence *vel non* of white specificity as a resolvable question of fact. The alternatives model emphasizes the context in which a challenged decision is made and views decisionmaking in a predominantly white environment with skepticism. Accordingly, this model presumes the race specificity of decisionmaking in such an environment. This presumption is merely a trigger for further analysis, however; the alternatives model is agnostic on the question whether there are in fact any facially race-neutral criteria of decision in a predominantly white decisionmaking context.

The two models also differ regarding the framework in which the issue of justification is to be resolved. Under the foreseeable impact model, this question arises under the heading of the business necessity defense or, if the employer makes the case that the assimilationist practice is a matter of business necessity, the plaintiff may propose an alternative that is not assimilationist but serves the employer's legitimate business objectives equally well. At bottom, these analyses turn on the question of the extent to which assimilation ought to be considered a matter of business necessity. Under the alternatives model, the plaintiff proposes alternative business practices without first confronting the question of business necessity. This model supplants the concept of business necessity with a notion of reasonable accommodation. Ultimately, however, each of these analytic schemes recognizes that in the realm of employment decisionmaking, criteria of selection that require assimilation to white-specific norms constitute "built-in headwinds" for nonwhite employees, and thus violate Title VII's proscription of employment actions taken "because of" race.[62] Because this fundamental statutory objective must inform each model, and because the same notion of assimilation animates both approaches, one should not anticipate different final outcomes due to differences in the way the two doctrines are framed.

The foreseeable impact model embodies a categorical approach to the problem of transparently white subjective decisionmaking with regard to both stages of the analysis—the questions of disparate impact and business necessity. That is, the decisionmaker must decide whether there *is* or *is not* a foreseeable impact, and whether a proven assimilationist practice *is* or *is not* justified as a matter of business necessity. This categorical style is attractive because it is conceptually familiar. It is a common form of legal analysis, and in the context of Title VII may gain some credibility because its structure parallels existing disparate impact doctrine. On the other hand, the weakness of the categorical approach is the way it implicitly categorizes groups as well as criteria of decision. Proof that a particular criterion of decision is in fact associated more closely with whites than with other racial groups seems inevitably to require a showing that the groups differ from one another in relevant respects, which in turn may implicate connotations of inferiority.

In contrast to this categorical style, the alternatives model reflects a skeptical and accommodationist attitude. It presumes the existence of racially disparate effects when certain structural conditions are met, and it imposes a requirement of reasonable accommodation that does not require categorical evaluation of what is or is not a matter of business necessity. The skeptical aspect of the alternatives model is relatively unfamiliar as a style of legal analysis, though it does have the virtue of responding in a fairly direct way to the transparency phenomenon.

The principal advantage of the foreseeable impact model is that it does a better job of preserving employer autonomy than does the alternatives model. The latter appears to require (possibly radical) restructuring of any white-dominated workplace whenever a nonwhite employee is added to the workforce. Because it is the workplace structure that triggers analysis of assimilationism, any nonwhite employee has the power to present alternative ways of doing things to which the employer must respond.[63] This relatively radical consequence may be mitigated somewhat by the fact that it is the plaintiff, rather than the employer, who must formulate the alternatives to be put on the table for consideration, but in the end every white employer in a predominantly white workplace would be forced to take seriously nonwhite employees' proposals for change. Because the foreseeable impact model does not allow the plaintiff to rely on a structural analysis of the workplace, but rather requires her to demonstrate the existence of foreseeable disparate effects, it does not intrude as deeply into employer prerogatives. Those attracted to the view that it is important to maintain a realm of private autonomy relatively insulated from public intrusion may favor the foreseeable impact approach because it does not threaten potentially overinclusive imposition of liability, as does the alternatives model.

On the other hand, the alternatives model also has its strengths. It does not carry the troubling moral implications of the foreseeable impact model's ascription of racial difference. Moreover, the alternatives approach avoids an institutional difficulty presented by the foreseeable impact model. Even if one overcomes one's resistance to the proposition that there are cultural differences tied to race that ought to be taken into account under Title VII, as I believe should be done, it is another matter to expect courts to resolve cases on the basis of a factual finding that such differences exist. Those who are especially concerned about either the moral or institutional problems of the foreseeable impact model may prefer the alternatives model. In sum, the two approaches present a normative dilemma: Should one prefer an approach that preserves a realm of decisionmaking autonomy for private employers, at the cost of institutionalizing the idea that there are significant cultural differences between the races, or should one opt for an approach that avoids the ascription of difference, at the cost of greater intrusion on employer prerogatives? My own conclusion is that institutional racism cannot be eliminated if the private sector is permitted to persist in excluding nonwhites from positions of power and authority; thus measures that "intrude" into the realm of "the private" are necessary if there is to be meaningful racial redistribution. From this perspective, then, the threatening countenance of the alternatives model may be the face of moral necessity. I leave it to the reader, however, to consider the question for herself.

[6]

Statutory Interpretation

B ECAUSE THE PROPOSALS discussed in chapter 5 implicate interpretation of a statute—Title VII—they
raise issues somewhat different from those addressed in chapter 4 concerning constitutional interpretation. However,
there are some parallels as well. Before implementing either
of the alternative models of Title VII liability, a court would
have to be persuaded that the statute's fundamental policy
regarding race discrimination encompasses discrimination in
the form of transparently white decisionmaking. Moreover,
some might argue that there is an issue of judicial role to be
addressed here too, though it does not loom nearly as large
as in the constitutional realm.

The Meaning of Title VII

Title VII prohibits "discrimination," but the statute leaves
obscure the precise meaning of that term. Its possible mean-

ings are most easily explored via a corollary—the concept of equality. That is, I understand "discrimination" as the failure to act in a manner consistent with workplace equality; the various senses of "discrimination" therefore correspond to the various senses of "equality" employed in this discussion. In outline, I argue here that Title VII, as amended by the Civil Rights Act of 1991, is no longer susceptible to what might be characterized as extreme "right-wing" and "left-wing" interpretations that rest respectively on symmetry-based and distributive conceptions of equality. By placing the disparate impact approach on a statutory foundation distinct from disparate treatment analysis, the 1991 Act implicitly ratified an equality principle that is more expansive than the notion of symmetrical treatment. At the same time, another provision added by the 1991 Act, which prohibits the use of race-normed employment tests, underscores Congress' long-standing rejection of a purely distributive conception of equality.[1] This stance can be traced back to section 703(j) of the 1964 Act, which insulated employers from liability for failure to maintain a racially balanced workplace.[2] Thus, the theoretical underpinnings of disparate impact liability must be found in the area between these two extremes—a region frequently described as implicating an "equal opportunity" notion of equality.

However, the concept of equal employment opportunity is itself subject to two interpretations, one pluralist and the other assimilationist. While the statute does not directly indicate which of these is the intended conception of equal opportunity, the general objectives of race neutrality and remedial redistribution that permeate the statutory scheme do provide indirect guidance. I argue that a pluralist understanding of equal opportunity more fully implements the underlying policies of Title VII than does the alternative, an assimilationist interpretation of equal opportunity.

As noted earlier, the disparate impact approach to Title VII liability was created through judicial interpretation in *Griggs v. Duke Power Co.*[3] The Supreme Court laid the theoretical foundation for this new approach as follows: "The objective of Congress in the enactment of Title VII . . . was to achieve equality of employment opportunities and remove barriers that have operated in the past to favor an identifiable group of white employees over other employees."[4] The Court then captured this general notion of equal opportunity in the image of " 'built-in headwinds' for minority groups."[5] Later doctrinal shifts that blurred the line between disparate impact analysis and proof of discriminatory intent may be understood as an attempt to rescind *Griggs*' opportunity-oriented theory in favor of a symmetry-based conception of equality. According to the latter, discrimination occurs if, and only if, some employees are treated differently from others because of race. Under this view, disparate impact analysis would be seen as an evidentiary mechanism designed to ferret out covert disparate treatment, including the pretextual use of facially neutral proxies for race. However, the purely symmetry-based interpretation of Title VII has been rendered implausible by Congress' clear endorsement of disparate impact as a distinct theory of liability, its finding that the *Wards Cove* decision "weakened the scope and effectiveness of Federal civil rights protections,"[6] and its concomitant rejection of the *Wards Cove* ruling on the business necessity defense.[7]

At the opposite extreme, it is evident that Congress never

has endorsed a purely distributive conception of equality in the workplace. The original version of Title VII contained a provision protecting employers from liability for failure to achieve racial balance in the workplace, and to date it has not been modified in any significant way.[8] The existence of this provision may account for what has been described as the Court's compromise in *Griggs:* The plaintiff may make out a prima facie case of discrimination by demonstrating a racial imbalance, but the employer may show that the imbalance is justified by proving that the criterion responsible for the disparate effect is related to job performance.[9] On a purely distributive conception of equality, of course, no such justification would be permitted. Moreover, the 1991 Act's prohibition against race-norming standardized tests strengthens the conclusion that undiluted distributive equality is not the objective at which the statute aims; race norming would promote distributive equality by ensuring that a standardized test would not have a disparate impact on the basis of race.

The foundation of the disparate impact approach, then, is neither the concept of symmetrical treatment nor a pure theory of distributive justice; it can be found instead in the notion of equal access. An employment practice that has an adverse impact on members of minority groups and that is unrelated to job requirements or business necessity creates an unnecessary barrier for members of those groups. This equal opportunity conception of equality differs from the equality-as-symmetry approach in that it recognizes that same treatment may not always remove race-specific barriers to achievement, and it diverges from the distributive conception of equality by ratifying disparate outcomes if they are the result of a process necessary to maintain business operations. Like the other two equality principles, however, the notion of equal opportunity is consistent with Title VII's proscription of employment practices that adversely affect individuals "because of" race.

The proposition that an opportunity-oriented principle of equality best explains the disparate impact theory of liability does not resolve the question whether Title VII ought to be read to provide a remedy for an employer's failure to take cultural diversity into account in making employment decisions. Equal opportunity might be understood as no more than the right of a nonwhite employee to play on an existing field, so that Keisha would have no cognizable complaint as long as she had the opportunity to conform to prevailing norms at her workplace. On the other hand, one might interpret equal opportunity as requiring alteration of the playing field itself in order to accommodate equally able players with diverse playing styles. On this interpretation, Keisha could argue that her employer should attempt to modify the workplace environment to conform to some degree to her cultural style, rather than placing the onus of adaptation on Keisha.

Of course, Congress has not explicitly stated which of these conceptions of equal employment opportunity is the correct interpretation of Title VII. However, consideration of two commonly recognized objectives of Title VII supports the conclusion that the pluralist interpretation is superior to the assimilationist approach. First, adopting the assimilationist interpretation—that equality means only an equal opportunity to compete on a preexisting field—fails to capture

Title VII's general goal of eliminating race as a factor in employment. Second, the pluralist conception of equal opportunity, which would require that the field be altered in order to accommodate cultural differences, is more fully aligned with the remedial goals of Title VII than is the assimilationist interpretation.

Under the assimilationist conception of equal employment opportunity, Keisha would be required to conform to the prevailing cultural norms in her dominantly white workplace at least to the extent that those norms implicate characteristics within her control. For example, grooming is generally thought to be a matter of personal choice, and to the extent that it is, each employee has an equal opportunity to conform to an employer's grooming code, regardless of race. The decisionmakers in Keisha's case could argue that she had been afforded an equal opportunity to conform to analogous, but more subtle, cultural norms.

This assimilationist position rests on a false dichotomy between race and individual choice. For Keisha, the two are inextricably intertwined because the aspects of personal identity implicated in the decision not to promote her are race-dependent. Thus the "choice" with which she is faced is in effect a choice to retain her racial identity as she understands it, or to renounce it. She would describe herself as having to shed or disavow crucial facets of blackness, if she wants to get ahead in her place of employment.

One might well argue in response, as could Keisha's supervisors, that even if Keisha experiences her personal qualities as linked with her race, in reality she has not been denied employment opportunity on the basis of race because she had the same chance as any white candidate to conform or be denied advancement. One cannot measure the subjective discomfort entailed by such a choice, the argument would go, and in any event subjective experience should not be relevant. Individuals must make all sorts of choices in life, including the choice whether to "fit in" to a particular environment. So long as the same demands are placed on all employees regardless of race, the argument continues, one should not say that race is a factor in a decision adversely affecting the individual who chooses not to conform.

The foregoing argument is problematic because it reiterates the transparency error. Because it underestimates the centrality of race to personal identity for people who are not white, it incorrectly assumes that the identity costs of conformity to the norms of a white cultural setting for a black person are commensurate with the identity costs incurred by a white person required to conform in the same setting.

Racial identity is not a central life experience for most white people, because it does not have to be. Like members of any socially dominant group, white people have the option to set aside consciousness of the characteristic that defines the dominant class—in this case, race. Thus whiteness is experienced as racelessness, and personal identity is conceived in a race-neutral manner. However, race plays quite a different role in the lives of people of color in this society. It is, again as a consequence of existing social structures that define and give meaning to racial identity, a central facet of life. One black feminist, bell hooks, describes her experience of race:

I often begin courses which focus on African-American literature, and sometimes specifically black women writers, with a declaration by Paulo Freire which had a profound liberatory effect on my thinking: "We cannot enter the struggle as objects in order to later become subjects." This statement compels reflection on how the dominated, the oppressed, the exploited make ourselves subject. How do we create an oppositional worldview, a consciousness, an identity, a standpoint that exists not only as that struggle which also opposes dehumanization but as that movement which enables creative, expansive self-actualization? Opposition is not enough. In that vacant space after one has resisted there is still the necessity to become—to make oneself anew. Resistance is that struggle we can most easily grasp. Even the most subjected person has moments of rage and resentment so intense that they respond, they act against. There is an inner uprising that leads to rebellion, however short-lived. It may be only momentary but it takes place. That space within oneself where resistance is possible remains. It is different then to talk about becoming subjects. That process emerges as one comes to understand how structures of domination work in one's own life, as one develops critical thinking and critical conscious-ness, as one invents new, alternative habits of being, and resists from that marginal space of difference inwardly defined.[10]

Thus, Keisha's employer is simply wrong in thinking that its conformity requirement is race-neutral; the standard places quite a different burden on nonwhites than it does on white employees. Moreover, this difference is not subjective, but structural. The social significance of race—the existence of a racial hierarchy—guarantees that race will intrude on the self-consciousness of nonwhites to an extent that most whites never will experience. Thus a "similarly situated" white candidate for promotion is unlikely to experience as race-dependent the personal attributes called into question by her employer's workplace conformity rule. Even if she does experience these attributes as associated with race, they are not likely to be *for that reason* central to her self-definition. For Keisha, on the other hand, conformity is excruciatingly difficult precisely because it calls her *racial* identity into question.

Once one sees that race is inevitably implicated in matters of "personal choice," it becomes apparent that the assimilationist interpretation does not truly reflect a conception of race-neutral employment opportunity. Under the assimilationist interpretation, the mandate of equality is satisfied in Keisha's case because she could, in theory, conform to the employer's expectations, even though doing so necessarily would levy costs on her that are inseparably linked to her race. The pluralist conception of equal opportunity embodies a more thoroughgoing notion of race neutrality. This interpretation of equality would not hold the requirements of equal opportunity to be satisfied unless the employer at least explored ways of accommodating diverse, race-dependent means of achieving legitimate business objectives. Thus only the pluralist interpretation of equal opportunity can capture fully the vision of a workplace in which race does not matter—in Title VII's language, a workplace in which the individual is not disadvantaged "because of" race.

Of course, Title VII's vision of race neutrality is closely tied to the redistributive objective of improving the relative economic position of blacks and other racial minorities. However, redistribution is not an end in itself; it is desirable because of a history of intentional discrimination and societal deprivation.[11] Thus, to the extent that Title VII aims at redistribution at all, it does so because of a remedial objective. Here too, the pluralist interpretation of equal opportunity emerges as a clearer expression of the Act's generic goals than does the assimilationist approach.

One consequence of two centuries of discrimination and disadvantage is that whites hold a disproportionate share of business ownership and decisionmaking power within corporate structures.[12] The assimilationist conception of equal employment opportunity does not address this persistent inequality, because it deems "equal" the opportunity to compete on this existing, though white-dominated, field. The pluralist interpretation of equality is a much more effective remedial tool because it requires an employer to restructure the workplace in ways that mitigate the effects of preexisting white dominance.

In sum, the two objectives of Title VII that often are perceived to conflict in the area of race-conscious "affirmative action" converge with regard to the concept of equal employment opportunity. Both race neutrality and remedial redistribution are more completely realized by interpreting equal employment opportunity in the pluralist, rather than assimilationist, sense. It seems fair, then, to conclude that fashioning a framework for assessing liability that would effectively accommodate Keisha's claim is consistent with Title VII as written.

The Principle of Judicial Restraint

Some might argue that asking the judiciary to implement either of the proposals set forth in chapter 5 is tantamount to asking the courts to repeat a crucial error embodied in *Griggs* itself—the error of judicial policymaking. In outline, this argument contends that the disparate impact model of liability was a judicial creation not authorized by the statute itself; such expansive interpretation takes the judiciary beyond its proper role into a realm that should be the exclusive province of the legislature—policy formation.[13] Clearly, this argument has a good deal in common with the contention that the courts ought to exercise restraint in constitutional interpretation because they are a "nondemocratic" institution.[14]

However, there are several significant differences between the statutory and constitutional contexts. First, when interpreting statutes courts generally have as their point of departure a text that is much more specific, much less open-ended, than a constitutional provision. Thus there is a framework for interpretive debate that leads more directly back to the "framers"—the legislature, in the case of statutes. Second, at least in the case of Title VII, one does not have to span a period of more than a century in the attempt to discern the "framers' " intent; the relevant group of initial policymakers is more or less the interpreters' contemporaries. Finally, and perhaps most significantly, courts' possible misinterpretations of statutes are more easily corrected by legislative action than are putative constitutional mistakes, which require the laborious process of constitutional amendment.

It also must be noted that the present proposals do not implicate the same degree of judicial "activism" as did creation of the disparate impact theory of liability in *Griggs*. Title VII, as amended in 1991, now clearly authorizes the disparate impact theory of liability; the proposals set forth here merely flesh out the evidentiary means through which a disparate impact case might be made in a case involving transparently white decisionmaking. Moreover, the statute's history and structure provide some theoretical guidance. As argued in the preceding section, they make it clear that disparate impact liability cannot be premised on either a purely symmetrical or a purely distributive conception of equality; the sole plausible candidate to fill the gap is a notion of equal opportunity. Thus, the current statute is unclear on only one point relevant to the present question—whether equal opportunity should be understood in a pluralist or an assimilationist sense.

Finally, Title VII addresses an area in which the legislature seems to have invited a degree of judicial "activism." Though disapproving *Wards Cove*, the 1991 Act relies on other judicial interpretations of Title VII, suggesting that on balance the legislature remains content to allow the judiciary to fill in gaps in the legislative scheme. The proposed interpretation of the Act—that Title VII should be read to incorporate a pluralist notion of equal opportunity—would constitute just such an interstitial enterprise, if undertaken by a court. Moreover, this interstitial interpretation does not rest on a court's own view of "sound public policy," but on the generic policies underlying the Act itself. The proposed pluralist interpretation of equal employment opportunity, then, ought to be seen as an exercise in mainstream statutory interpretation.[15]

[7]

Notes on Doctrinal Reform

THE PROPOSED TRANSPARENCY-CONSCIOUS modifications of Equal Protection and Title VII doctrines give rise to several jurisprudential considerations. First, they embody a more constructive discourse of responsibility, in place of the existing discourse of blame. Second, they implicate the problem of legal indeterminacy: If doctrine does not genuinely constrain legal decisionmakers, doctrinal reform seems an empty exercise. Finally, the project of reforming race discrimination law can benefit the larger enterprise of constructing an antiracist white identity.

Blame and Responsibility

Both of the doctrines under examination here—the constitutional requirement of discriminatory intent and Title VII's existing disparate impact rule—reflect a practice of blaming "violators" for discriminatory practices. However, the discourse of blame and punishment is not well suited to the task of racial remediation. An alternative more likely to have salutary consequences is a discourse of responsibility; that framework provides a theoretical foundation for the doctrinal proposals that have been presented here.

As I use it here, the notion of "blame" has two components: An act is blameworthy if it is both morally wrong and divergent from normal practice. Thus the constitutional requirement of discriminatory intent implicates "blameworthiness" insofar as it carries connotations of criminal liability: Heightened scrutiny is triggered only if there is a "bad actor" who has selected a course of action *because of* its adverse impact on nonwhites. In mainstream (liberal white) discourse today, deliberately setting out to disadvantage members of racial minority groups is both morally wrong and not the usual practice.

It is perhaps not equally obvious that existing Title VII disparate impact rules participate too in a discourse of blaming. However, when one looks at the requirements for establishing the existence of disparate effects, one has the sense that the courts want to be shown that a *particular* employer's *particular* criterion of selection is *the* cause of a demonstrated disparate effect. The constellation of requirements centering on actual disparate effects and tight lines of causation are quite reminiscent of the "intent" model of liability that is embodied in the constitutional rule. In this way, Title VII does incorporate the notion that legal liability is to be imposed only upon those who have stepped outside the bounds of accepted and acceptable practice.

Blaming is not an effective, empirically well-founded, or

prudent way of addressing the complete range of contemporary manifestations of race discrimination. The ineffectiveness of blaming becomes clear when one focuses attention on unconscious discrimination (of which transparently white decisionmaking is one form). In a simplified universe of only conscious and unconscious discrimination, there are three plausible approaches to assigning blameworthiness: society might label conscious, but not unconscious, discrimination, blameworthy; label both blameworthy; or label neither blameworthy. Brief reflection reveals that none of these approaches is likely effectively to address contemporary American forms of racial discrimination.

The position that conscious discrimination is blameworthy but unconscious discrimination is not, is counterproductive of the ultimate goal of racial justice. Disapproving only conscious racism provides an incentive for whites to repress and deny whatever racist attitudes they in fact harbor. As Charles Lawrence has explained, psychoanalytic theory posits that individuals respond to conflicts between social norms that condemn racist attitudes and beliefs and their own racist ideas by excluding the latter from conscious recognition.[1] Thus, norms that label only conscious discrimination as blameworthy may be counterproductive, as they may operate primarily to perpetuate racist attitudes in a relatively intractable form. In addition, focusing disapproval on the more blatant forms of discrimination may create a climate of backlash and denial: "*I* certainly am not a racist: *I* would not do these things."[2]

To hold both unconscious and conscious race discrimination equally blameworthy is also unlikely to produce desirable consequences. First, blaming individuals for unconsciously held attitudes may produce paralyzing guilt when the racist character of those attitudes comes to light. Furthermore, condemning the individual for matters not within his conscious control seems inconsistent with the concept of moral wrong associated with blaming. Finally, assessing blame for what, in effect, nearly every white person does seems equally incongruous; it is inconsistent with the notion that blame may attach only to actions outside the bounds of common practice.

The final option is to regard both conscious and unconscious race discrimination as morally acceptable. There is merit in the proposition that race neutrality is at least an overblown norm; race consciousness may not be the overarching evil it often seems to be. But there should be no doubt about the moral status of the end to which race consciousness historically has been directed: white supremacy. To dismiss too easily the immorality of race-conscious decisionmaking, in a framework in which concepts of blame and innocence remain operative, would be to allow the inference that white domination of blacks is an acceptable social outcome.

Blaming is not an empirically well-founded practice in the context of modern race discrimination. The transparency phenomenon casts doubt on a fundamental presupposition of the discourse of blame: that there exists a nonblameworthy alternative to the conduct for which blame is assessed. To say that either the conscious or unconscious use of race-specific criteria of decision is blameworthy is to suppose that some race-neutral alternative course of action might have been pursued instead. The lesson of transparency, however, is that in all likelihood race always is a factor influencing decisions that affect persons. To label one course of conduct blameworthy when there is no available "innocent" alternative seems simply unjust.

Finally, judicial reliance on unstated notions of blame, violation, and remedy is imprudent because the aura of criminality surrounding these concepts undoubtedly increases courts' resistance to imposing liability in circumstances that otherwise might call for it. With respect to constitutional doctrine, federal courts understandably hesitate to suggest that another branch of government has engaged in criminal conduct. With regard to Title VII, there is a similar, if perhaps less stubborn, reluctance to impose liability on a private employer who is not the sole cause of a given racially disproportionate outcome. However, such hesitation contributes to the maintenance of an unjust racial status quo. In a nonblaming framework, courts might become more effective participants in the effort to address and eradicate all forms of race discrimination.

The alternative to a discourse of blaming is a discourse of responsibility. In this model, one takes responsibility for correcting undesirable states of affairs without thereby accepting either blame for, or even a causal connection with, the circumstance that requires correction:

Notice first that to take responsibility for a state of affairs is not to claim responsibility for having caused it. So, for example, if I take responsibility for cleaning up the kitchen I am not thereby admitting to any role in creating the mess; the state of the kitchen may be the consequence of actions quite independent of me.[3]

The kitchen example is apt for the dimension of fault as well as causation: Even if I have had a hand in creating the mess in the kitchen, the blameworthiness *vel non* of my past conduct is not relevant to the commitment to change the existing state of affairs that taking responsibility entails.

Any white decisionmaker can choose to take responsibility for the form of unconscious race discrimination "transparency" describes by adopting a skeptical stance with respect to seemingly race-neutral criteria of decision she employs. Deliberate skepticism regarding race neutrality permits the decisionmaker to step outside the framework of blame and guilt that rarely offers more than a choice between legitimation of the status quo and paralysis.[4] For government and private-employer decisionmakers, legally imposed deliberate skepticism provides an avenue for addressing unconscious discrimination while circumventing the problems of blaming described above.

The constitutional proposal set forth in chapter 3 states that a special form of heightened scrutiny should be triggered by *any* government action with racially disparate effects. That scrutiny focuses on whether government wishes to justify a particular course of action by reference to an assimilationist objective, and, if that is not the case, whether adequately pluralist means are employed in pursuit of a nonassimilationist goal. This proposal implements government responsibility for race discrimination in two ways. First, it sends the message that government is unwilling to leave the racial "kitchen" in a mess, whether or not the mess is the government's creation. Though the proposed rule pressures government to behave in a nonassimilationist manner, it is not a matter of external coercion: Adopting the proposed rule amounts to one branch—the judiciary—binding the other branches (and, presumably, itself) to a pluralist interpretation of the guarantee of equal protection. This scenario is most like one in which a group appoints one member to assign individual responsibilities; the designated decisionmaker then concludes that each of the members (including herself) ought to clean the kitchen whenever it is a mess. In a sense, the *entire group* has taken responsibility for kitchen messes.

Second, the proposed constitutional rule implements government responsibility for race discrimination with respect to the bottom line: One can expect more pluralist decisionmaking in a regime governed by the proposed rule than under the existing requirement of discriminatory intent. At a minimum, the proposal transfers some decisionmaking authority to members of racial minority groups: They may set forth means of achieving government's articulated goals that *must* be adopted unless government can show them to be less effective than the means government would prefer to employ. One can only assume that government will be unable to meet that standard some of the time, and so will be required to alter its otherwise desired course of action. This constitutes an instance of government responsibility for racism if, and to the extent that, it actually results in racial redistribution, just as taking responsibility for cleaning the kitchen is something that has taken place only if, and to the extent that, the kitchen ends up clean.

In the Title VII realm, it is not as clear that adopting either the foreseeable effects or alternatives models of disparate impact liability can be analogized to the situation of an individual who takes responsibility for a kitchen mess she did not create, because here it cannot be said that government is binding itself. As applied to private employers, an interpretation of Title VII that mandates pluralist decisionmaking in the workplace constitutes government coercion of private conduct. It might seem that the private employer is forced to clean a kitchen mess that may have been made by others.

Nevertheless, the situation of the private employer required by Title VII to employ pluralist criteria of decision can be understood as an instance of taking responsibility—collective responsibility—for institutional racism. First, because the proposed models of liability are not linked to causation and actual disparate effects, they depart from the current rule's connotation of blameworthiness. Second, because whites are the dominant group in this society, there is a sense in which any law that benefits people of color amounts to whites constraining ourselves. Here members of a group bind themselves in a manner that encompasses even those individuals who otherwise might not be inclined to take a role in cleaning the kitchen. Whites as a group cannot be said to have taken responsibility for white privilege if we endorse a regime that leaves some whites free to continue to benefit from that privilege.

Third, as noted with respect to the constitutional proposal, the core of the notion of responsibility is practical outcomes; (some)one has taken responsibility if, and only if, the kitchen ends up clean. Like the constitutional proposal, the foreseeable effects and alternatives models of Title VII liability aim at racial redistribution, regardless of what forces in fact account for the existing inequitable state of affairs. To that extent, they too implement a responsibility-based approach to antidiscrimination law.

Suppose, then, that one asks this question: Even accepting that taking responsibility for racial injustice is a good thing, what is the justification for making such responsibility a matter of law? I think there are two answers to this question. First, law embodies a society's norms. Thus rules that impose responsibility on government and private employers for transparently white decisionmaking would send a message that we are no longer willing to overlook that vehicle of racial oppression. More generally, that course of action would send a message that we expect individuals as well as government to take responsibility in matters of racial injustice. Second, and in my view more importantly, rules disapproving transparently white decisionmaking have the potential to alter the existing distribution of social and material wealth. We ask everyone to take responsibility for this particular mess so that, no matter what the actual cause, it really does get cleaned up.

Does Doctrine Constrain?

The proposition that the doctrinal reforms proposed in chapters 3 and 5 could assist in the racial redistribution of social goods depends in part on an assumption about the ability of legal doctrines generally to determine legal outcomes. That is, the enterprise of doctrinal reform apparently presupposes belief in the efficacy of doctrine itself; if doctrine does not determine outcomes, then it makes no sense to modify doctrine in an effort to achieve a set of outcomes different from those currently available.

The thesis that law is radically indeterminate—that doctrine alone never is dispositive of legal outcomes, such that any result is possible in any case—generally is associated with the Critical Legal Studies movement.[5] In brief, the indeterminacy thesis contends that the legal decisionmaker always has available a range of culturally plausible rationales that would support contrary outcomes. The specific argument techniques that make such outcomes possible vary from case to case. In one instance, conflicting norms or fundamental principles might come into play, in another the decisionmaker might have a choice to make between competing policies or rules, or a rule and its exceptions. In some legal settings competing techniques of interpretation are available; they too provide an avenue for the formulation of legal analyses reaching diametrically opposite conclusions. In any event, the indeterminacy thesis claims, there always is available some analytic maneuver that would make any desired result seem respectable.

The doctrines examined in this book provide an illustration of the indeterminacy thesis. I argued in chapter 3 that the constitutional requirement of discriminatory intent fails to respond to the transparency phenomenon, and that a rule applying heightened, transparency-conscious scrutiny to all government actions that have racially disparate effects would be a more satisfactory legal approach to the problem. However, there is no inherent guarantee that the proposed rule would achieve its intended objective. As noted earlier, absent vigilant attention to the transparency phenomenon, the proposed rule could permit reinstitution of transparency in another form by validating transparently white, or assimilationist, government purposes.[6]

Moreover, even supposing this pitfall were avoided, the operation of disparate impact analysis in the Title VII context reveals another set of perils connected with the proof of disparate effects. As Keisha's case shows, such rules can evolve in ways that limit their effectiveness as a remedy for transparently white decisionmaking. Thus, in chapter 5 I set forth two alternatives that would avoid or ameliorate most of the weaknesses in the existing rules. Even here, however, there are hazards. For example, an employer might contest a claim of differential impact by pointing to a subgroup of nonwhites having roughly the same distribution as whites of the relevant characteristic.[7] Such an approach again would function to reinstate assimilationism.

In sum, neither adopting a disparate effects approach to transparency-driven discrimination, nor any particular method of proving disparate effects, provides absolute assurance that transparently white norms will be displaced in practice. For many commentators, this degree of legal indeterminacy is not problematic, though for others it presents a challenge to the legitimacy of the legal system as a whole.[8] However, the significance of the indeterminacy thesis for the present project is more limited and more pragmatic: What value is there in proposing new doctrinal approaches if they carry no assurance of efficacy?

I respond to the indeterminacy difficulty by conceiving legal doctrine as a sort of promise. Webster's dictionary defines a "promise" as "a declaration that one will do or refrain from doing something specified," and indicates as well that a promise is "a declaration that gives the person to whom it is made a right to expect or to claim the performance or forbearance of a specified act."[9] Thus when I promise to mow the lawn this Saturday, I am assuring the promisee that I intend to mow, and creating the expectation that I will indeed do so.

Here, I rely upon the model of the gratuitous promise (a promise made in the absence of any reciprocal promise or expectation of return), rather than contract (in which there is a bargained-for exchange). The difference, of course, is that the former, unlike the latter, is not legally enforceable. Indeed, I have in mind the sort of gratuitous promise whose breach carries no adverse consequences at all to the promisor, other than the weight of moral failure and/or the disappointed expectations of the promisee (I assume there has been no detrimental reliance on the part of the promisee). Even in this case, promising is possible, and it is this circumstance that poses most clearly the question whether, and in what sense, promising constrains the promisor.

Consider again the lawn mowing example. If I make no declaration at all, I create no expectation regarding whether or when I will mow. The nature of promising is such that saying "I promise . . ." alters the situation at least to the extent that an expectation has been created. Moreover, different promises create different expectations. I might have promised to do some yard work on Saturday, without specifying precisely what tasks I would perform, or I might have promised to mow "sometime," or "next weekend," without being more exact about the date. From the perspective of the promisee, it matters that I have promised, and it matters what I have promised.

Of course, gratuitous promises that do not induce detrimental reliance make a difference to the promisor only to the extent he or she feels bound to keep his or her promises. But language analysts often have noted that the practice of promising would not exist were it common for promisors not to keep their word.[10] Thus it is intrinsic to the notion of promise that promising constrains the future action of the promisor. Because promising constrains, different promises constrain differently.

Legal doctrine can be conceived as a sort of promise. Government is the promisor; individuals are the promisees. In general, both criminal and civil laws can be thought of in this way, though they do not necessarily conform to the "promising" model in every respect. In a sense, government promises freedom from prosecution to persons who do not violate its criminal statutes; similarly, government promises intervention or not in individuals' affairs in accordance with the civil laws. When people form expectations because of, and conform their conduct to, legal rules, they are in much the same position as any ordinary promisee.

But, one might object, government's promises are enforceable, and thus are unlike the gratuitous promises described above. However, even if one accepts the idea that the relation between the government and the individual is more like a contract than a gratuitous promise, the fact of legal indeterminacy casts doubt on the thesis that individuals genuinely have remedies when government fails to keep its promises.

Legal indeterminacy means that laws are similar to vague promises (that is, promises whose content is unclear). A legal claimant always faces a risk that the law's interpreter will construe government's promise differently than does the claimant; in effect, the interpreter declares, "What you ask is not what was promised." Thus, by virtue of inherent linguistic indeterminacy, government indeed is in a position much like that of the gratuitous promisor: The consequences of breach are limited to the promisor's own sense of responsibility and the promisee's disappointed expectations.

Do vague promises constrain? Certainly there is a point at which an assurance of future conduct is so vague as to provide no "right to expect . . . performance." I label such a declaration an empty promise. For example, "I'll mow the lawn sometime" may be an empty promise in the absence of implicit qualifications such as "before it's a foot high." But there is a continuum of indefiniteness, and other promises may be subject to varying interpretation and yet constrain. For instance, people use "next weekend" differently: On Wednesday, "next weekend" may refer to the first succeeding weekend, or to the second. Thus "I'll mow next weekend" may not be quite clear on its face, but it is specific with respect to any given interpretation of "next," and so a promise has been made. Indeterminate content does not necessarily defeat the claim that promises constrain.

One need not resolve the question whether any particular doctrine is in fact empty—so vague as to be meaningless—or merely indeterminate to find value in the enterprise of doctrinal reform. The notion of doctrine as promise envisages legal rules as relational; assessing the content of doctrine requires considering both the respective points of view of the promisor and the promisee. If a given rule is susceptible to multiple interpretations, comparing these points of view may provide a means of selecting the interpretation that ought to control. Even if one accepts the contention of some Critical Legal scholars that some—or all—doctrines are tantamount to empty promises, the notion of promising provides a framework in which to argue that it's possible to do better. In daily life, promisors are capable of making promises they can keep, and of articulating those promises in relatively clear, comprehensible terms that provide a reasonable basis for expectation. I don't believe it has been demonstrated that law's creators and interpreters are inherently unable to do as well.

The notion of doctrine as promise situates the enterprise of doctrinal reform as an exercise in sorting out what was (or should be) promised by whom to whom, and thus what it means to keep a particular promise as embodied in legal language. Such promises may be seen as gratuitous and often vague, but they nevertheless constrain the responsible promisor in much the same way that everyday promises constrain. Doctrinal reform matters because the content of even unenforceable promises matters.

The constitutional requirement of discriminatory intent promises little in the way of addressing race discrimination, because it singles out a relatively small segment of the full spectrum of racist behavior. Moreover, because it is very difficult to establish that government acted with discriminatory intent—it must have selected a course of conduct "because of, not merely in spite of" its racially disparate effects—the promise to provide a legal sanction for race discrimination is in this instance tantamount to an empty promise.

Title VII promises somewhat more, in that it does provide a remedy for disparate impact discrimination. However, the complexity of existing rules regarding proof of disparate effects means that the implicit promise to provide a remedy for unconscious discrimination, and specifically for transparently white decisionmaking, is in practice unlikely to be kept. In effect, the apparent promise of Title VII disparate impact analysis is a little white lie.

In contrast to the existing constitutional and Title VII rules, the proposals set forth here promise more: They promise to create a pluralistic government and workplace, and in so doing they carry a promise that whites will share the goods associated with a privileged position in society. Of course, the indeterminacy thesis says that these promises too may not be kept; that there is no way to construct a legal doctrine that can guarantee delivery on the promises it makes. Nevertheless, I find a value in promising more rather than less.

Doctrine and White Identity

White privilege is a "package of unearned assets . . . an invisible weightless knapsack of special provisions, assurance, tools, maps, guides, codebooks, passports, visas, clothes, compass, emergency gear, and blank checks." [11] Transparency is one aspect of white privilege: It is the privilege of not having to notice one's privilege. [12] If transparency defines whiteness, the whiteness it defines is privilege unmodified.

An antiracist white identity is one that (among other things) is aware of, and attempts to renounce, white privilege. I believe the first step in the process of developing such an identity is to overcome the habit of transparency; that is, to develop the habit of seeing oneself as explicitly white, and of identifying seemingly neutral norms as white. Admittedly, because transparently white norms carry positive connotations, the move to become conscious of whiteness could be perilous: It risks reinforcing "negative" stereotypes of nonwhites.[13] Nevertheless, firm attention to the ultimate objective of an antiracist white identity—racial redistribution— should reduce that peril. A genuinely antiracist white identity is pluralist; it demands that one value nonwhite racial identities as well.

The examination of race discrimination law undertaken here sheds light on white privilege by exposing the assumptions upon which existing race discrimination law rests. As described earlier, both the constitutional requirement of discriminatory intent and Title VII's disparate impact rule envision racism as a blameworthy departure from a normal state of affairs in which race plays no role. This vision is characteristically white; it embodies the white privilege of accepting as a baseline for thought and action the proposition that race does not matter. Similarly, the failure of Equal Protection law and Title VII to take account of the transparency phenomenon reflects the white attitude that what appears to be race neutral must be so in fact. This facet of race discrimination law illustrates definitive white carelessness about the salience of race.

Even if one does not undertake an active role in the effort to change antidiscrimination law, reflection on transparency in the context of these legal doctrines can contribute to the development of an antiracist white identity. Contemplating the ways existing law reflects and reinforces white privilege, and the ways it might be modified to contest that privilege, is one part of a larger project of awareness that is an essential element of antiracist whiteness. We cannot combat structures of privilege of which we are unaware, and in some circumstances awareness itself erodes privilege.

However, though raising one's consciousness of white privilege is a necessary ingredient in developing an antiracist whiteness, it is not nearly sufficient. Acquiescing in the status quo has the existential effect of constructing the self as a white supremacist, though perhaps one who occupies that position unconsciously. White people must make concrete efforts to renounce white privilege and to foster racial redistribution. We must find ways to share wealth, power, and prestige with nonwhites. The place to begin constructing a genuinely nonracist white identity is at the point where whites really give up something.

Systems of privilege are so complex and interwoven into society that it is no easy matter to formulate effective redistributive strategies. Some commentators, including Ian Haney López, recommend that white people *abandon* whiteness.[14] However, this proposal assumes a capacity the privileged may not have. Because privilege is conferred, not adopted or earned, it cannot be abandoned unilaterally. Thus a strategy of abandonment may be more symbolic than real.

It seems to me that one alternative is to consciously employ white privilege to the advantage of nonwhites. (Of course the individual or group doing so must not seek gratitude or return, or the act could not foster racial redistribution.) For example, whites in a position to do so might appoint as judges only people of color. Analogously, whites who have input into the process of doctrinal formation can advocate legal rules that might effect greater racial justice, such as the proposals set forth here.

This approach—using privilege in an antiracist manner— must be adopted with extreme caution. Retaining privilege is too attractive, too comfortable, to provide assurance that the privileged are in a good position to evaluate when and whether renouncing privilege is a realistic option. Thus, it might be argued that the conception of the white person as the promisor, the author of race discrimination law, is not well considered, because it sustains the image of whites as those who wield power in society. By way of comparison, doctrinal proposals that make nonwhites the final arbiters of legal outcomes offer a more complete transfer of power and authority.[15]

However, the reality is that white people do control the formation and application of legal doctrines at this time. Is renunciation of that status possible? The most direct method would be simply to hand to nonwhites authority over doctrinal formulation and interpretation, but this approach likely would entail too much change too quickly even for most whites of good will. A less complete, but arguably more feasible approach would follow the strategy sketched here: that we develop legal doctrines that create legal remedies for all the forms in which institutional racism manifests itself. Creating effective legal measures to counteract transparently white decisionmaking is one part of that agenda. Though the power to impose white norms on nonwhites, even unwittingly, is surely not the sole form of power whites should relinquish, yielding that power is an important component of any antiracist white agenda. Constructing legal doctrines that promise to bring the pressure of government to bear against the practice of transparently white decisionmaking, then, is an exercise in binding ourselves to give up one facet of white supremacy.

Notes

1. Neil Gotanda calls this the technique of nonrecognition. Racial identity must first be recognized, then suppressed, so that race is "noticed, but not considered." Neil Gotanda, *A Critique of "Our Constitution is Color-Blind,"* 44 STAN. L. REV. 1, 16–18 (1991).

2. I focus on blacks as the group most centrally affected by white supremacy for two principal reasons. First, the dynamics of blacks' oppression are unique, as evidenced, for example, by the institutions of slavery and racial apartheid, which provide the core definition of race discrimination in this society. Second, I would like to encourage white readers to reexamine our habit of thinking of race discrimination as a monolithic phenomenon, and to reflect on the different forms it may take with respect to different nonwhite racial groups, issues, and circumstances. To remind the reader that some, but certainly not all, of what I say about blacks applies equally to other racial groups, I intermittently will substitute nonwhite for black in the text. See Neil Gotanda, *"Other Non-Whites" in American Legal History,* 85 COLUM. L. REV. 1186 (1985) (reviewing PETER IRONS, JUSTICE AT WAR (1983)) (arguing that analysis of issues as they affect nonblack racial minorities should differ from analysis with respect to blacks).

I have chosen not to capitalize black, for reasons that are, paradoxically, related to Kim Crenshaw's reason for doing so. In her view, "Blacks, like Asians, Latinos, and other 'minorities,' constitute a specific cultural group and, as such, require denotation as a proper noun." Kimberlé W. Crenshaw, *Race, Reform, and Retrenchment: Transformation and Legitimation in Antidiscrimination Law,* 101 HARV. L. REV. 1331, 1332 n.2 (1988). However, part of the agenda for this article is to encourage white people to break free from our tendency to associate race with people of color, and to develop instead a positive racial awareness of whiteness. Accordingly, I think it most appropriate here either to capitalize both black and white, or to capitalize neither, and, in the interest of defusing potential charges of essentialism, I have opted for the latter.

3. Some social scientists have recognized and discussed this phenomenon. See Robert W. Terry, *The Negative Impact on White Values,* in IMPACTS OF RACISM ON WHITE AMERICANS 119, 120 (Benjamin P. Bowser & Raymond G. Hunt eds., 1981) ("To be white in America is not to have to think about it.") (emphasis omitted); Judy H. Katz & Allen Ivey, *White Awareness: The Frontier of Racism Awareness Training,* 55 PERSONNEL & GUIDANCE J. 485, 486 (1977) ("White people do not see themselves as white.") (emphasis omitted). Janet Helms concludes: "it appears that most Whites have no consistent conception of a positive White identity or consciousness. As a consequence, Whites may feel threatened by the actual or presupposed presence of racial consciousness in non-White racial groups." Janet E. Helms, *Toward a Model of White Racial Identity Development,* in BLACK AND WHITE RACIAL IDENTITY 50 (Janet E. Helms ed., 1990).

However, I do not rest my implicit claim that the transparency phenomenon is "real"—a good way of conceptualizing things—primarily on the authority of social scientists, in part because they too must rely at bottom on the reported experience of white people. More importantly, I believe we are more likely to take transparency seriously if we recognize it in our own lives than if our only acquaintance with it is third-hand "empirical" evidence.

4. Pat Cain reports that in her experience white women never include whiteness as one of the three adjectives. See Patricia A. Cain, *Feminist Jurisprudence: Grounding the Theories,* 4 BERKELEY WOMEN'S L.J. 191, 208 (1989–90).

5. Ruth Frankenberg collects and describes white women's experience of whiteness in RUTH FRANKENBERG, WHITE WOMEN, RACE MATTERS: THE SOCIAL CONSTRUCTION OF WHITENESS (1993).

6. This distinction is described in more detail in chapter 2.

7. On pluralism, see Gerald Torres, *Critical Race Theory: The Decline of the Universalist Idea; and the Hope of Plural Justice—Some*

Observations and Questions of an Emerging Phenomenon, 75 MINN. L. REV. 993 (1991).

8. Some racist institutions are based overtly on racial hostility; others are based on egalitarian norms but nevertheless produce racially skewed results. Institutional racism is described more completely in chapter 2. Because existing laws do recognize animus-based discrimination, they can provide some relief from institutional practices that are the product of racial animus.

9. See Richard Delgado, *The Ethereal Scholar: Does Critical Legal Studies Have What Minorities Want?* 22 HARV. C.R.-C.L. L. REV. 301, 315 (1987) ("A society that enacts rules and provides structures to curb racism announces that racism is unacceptable behavior. By committing ourselves to norms of fairness we become fairer people.")

10. Especially helpful analyses of "affirmative action" include Cheryl Harris, *Whiteness as Property,* 106 HARV. L. REV. 1707 (1993); Thomas Ross, *Innocence and Affirmative Action,* 43 VAND. L. REV. 297 (1990).

11. See, e.g., RICHARD A. EPSTEIN, SIMPLE RULES FOR A COMPLEX WORLD (1995).

12. Katzenbach v. Morgan, 384 U.S. 641 (1966).

13. See RICHARD KLUGER, SIMPLE JUSTICE: THE HISTORY OF *BROWN V. BOARD OF EDUCATION* AND BLACK AMERICA'S STRUGGLE FOR EQUALITY (1975); Ruth Bader Ginsburg & Barbara Flagg, *Some Reflections on the Feminist Legal Thought of the 1970s,* 1989 U. CHI. LEGAL F. 9.

NOTES TO CHAPTER 2

1. Masatoshi Nei & Arun K. Roychoudhury, *Genetic Relationship and Evolution of Human Races,* 14 EVOLUTIONARY BIOLOGY 1, 11 (1982); L. KAMIN, R. LEWONTIN, & STEPHEN ROSE, NOT IN OUR GENES: BIOLOGY, IDEOLOGY, AND HUMAN NATURE (1984); Alan Almquist & John Cronin, *Fact, Fancy and Myth on Human Evolution,* 29 CURRENT ANTHROPOLOGY 520 (1988).

2. The U.S. Supreme Court upheld the law requiring segregated

railroad cars, and the doctrine of "separate but equal," in Plessy v. Ferguson, 163 U.S. 537 (1896). It is not certain whether the conductor recognized Plessy or had been told about him; Richard Kluger suggests that the encounter was prearranged to test the segregation statute. RICHARD KLUGER, SIMPLE JUSTICE: THE HISTORY OF *BROWN V. BOARD OF EDUCATION* AND BLACK AMERICA'S STRUGGLE FOR EQUALITY 73 (1975).

3. MARVIN HARRIS, PATTERNS OF RACE IN THE AMERICAS 58–59 (1964).

4. *Id.* at 59.

5. Ian F. Haney López, *The Social Construction of Race: Some Observations on Illusion, Fabrication, and Choice,* 29 HARV. C.R.-C.L. L. REV. 1, 28 (1994).

6. *Id.* at 44–45.

7. For contemporary accounts of race's plasticity, see JUDY SCALES-TRENT, NOTES OF A WHITE BLACK WOMAN: RACE, COLOR, COMMUNITY (1995); PATRICIA J. WILLIAMS, *On Being the Object of Property,* in THE ALCHEMY OF RACE AND RIGHTS: DIARY OF A LAW PROFESSOR 216 (1991).

8. ANDREW HACKER, TWO NATIONS 93–106 (1992); U.S. BUREAU OF THE CENSUS, STATISTICAL ABSTRACT OF THE UNITED STATES: 1991, at 38, 386 (1991).

9. See Richard J. Lazarus, *Pursuing "Environmental Justice": The Distributional Effects of Environmental Protection,* 87 NW. U. L. REV. (1993).

10. Hacker, *supra* note 8, at 231.

11. See JONATHAN KOZOL, SAVAGE INEQUALITIES: CHILDREN IN AMERICA'S SCHOOLS (1991).

12. Hacker, *supra* note 8, at 107–12, 234.

13. See, e.g., STATISTICAL ABSTRACT, *supra* note 8, at 454 (reporting that median income of whites increased almost 10 percent from $32,713 in 1970 to $35,975 in 1989; for blacks the 1970 median was $20,067 and in 1989 only $20,209, an increase of less than 1 percent).

14. See Adarand Constructors, Inc. v. Pena, 515 U.S. 200 (1995)(applying strict scrutiny to all race-specific classifications, includ-

ing those designed to remedy past discrimination); see also DERRICK A. BELL, JR., AND WE ARE NOT SAVED 123–39 (1987).

15. IAN F. HANEY LÓPEZ, WHITE BY LAW: THE LEGAL CONSTRUCTION OF RACE 43–44 (1996).

16. *Id.* at 5–9.

17. "In signifying race, a person having one-thirty second or less of negro blood shall not be deemed, described, or designated by any public official in the state of Louisiana as "colored," a "mulatto," a "black," a "negro," a "griffe," an "Afro-American," a "quadroon," a "mestizo," a "colored person" or a "person of color." LA. REV. STAT. ANN. 42:267 (Enacted 1970 La. Acts No. 46, repealed 1983 La. Acts No. 441).

18. Calvin Trillin, *American Chronicles: Black or White,* NEW YORKER, April 14, 1986, at 62.

19. These themes are elaborated in chapter 7.

20. Patricia G. Devine, *Stereotypes and Prejudice: Their Automatic and Controlled Components,* 56 J. PERSONALITY & SOCIAL PSYCHOLOGY 5 (1989).

21. Dr. Thomas Pettigrew, quoted in Daniel Coleman, *"Useful" Modes of Thinking Contribute to the Power of Prejudice,* N.Y. TIMES, May 12, 1987, at C1, C10.

22. Charles Lawrence describes this type of thinking as "repressed hostility." Charles R. Lawrence III, *The Id, the Ego, and Equal Protection: Reckoning with Unconscious Racism,* 39 STAN. L. REV. 317 (1987).

23. Patricia G. Devine et al., *Prejudice with and without Compunction,* 60 J. PERSONALITY & SOCIAL PSYCHOLOGY 817, 817–19 (1991).

24. *Id.*

25. David Wellman contends that an egalitarian ideology may be an integral component of institutional racism. DAVID WELLMAN, PORTRAITS OF WHITE RACISM 54–62 (2d ed. 1993).

26. See Robert Friedman, *Institutional Racism: How to Discriminate without Really Trying,* in RACIAL DISCRIMINATION IN THE UNITED STATES 384, 388–91 (Thomas F. Pettigrew ed., 1975).

27. *Id.* at 392–93.

NOTES TO CHAPTER 3

1. Bolling v. Sharpe, 347 U.S. 497 (1954).

2. 347 U.S. 483 (1954).

3. 426 U.S. 229 (1976).

4. 401 U.S. 424 (1971).

5. The Court of Appeals decision is reported at Davis v. Washington, 512 F.2d 956 (D.C. Cir. 1975), *rev'd.*, Washington v. Davis, 426 U.S. 229 (1976). The Court of Appeals opinion has as an appendix the full text of Test 21. 512 F.2d at 967–76.

6. The *Griggs* opinion reads: "The Act proscribes not only overt discrimination but also practices that are fair in form, but discriminatory in operation. The touchstone is business necessity. If an employment practice which operates to exclude Negroes cannot be shown to be related to job performance, the practice is prohibited." 401 U.S. at 431. The Court elaborated: "[G]ood intent or absence of discriminatory intent does not redeem employment procedures or testing mechanisms that operate as 'built-in headwinds' for minority groups and are unrelated to measuring job capability." 401 U.S. at 432. The language seems reasonably straightforward: Intent is no part of a disparate impact claim. However, chiefly because the facts of the case strongly suggested that the employer had adopted the challenged facially neutral job requirements as a pretext for discrimination, some have read the *Griggs* disparate impact approach to provide no more than an indirect method of proving discriminatory intent. The interpretation of *Griggs* will be addressed in greater detail in chapter 6.

7. *Davis,* 426 U.S. at 238.

8. This phrase originates with Gerald Gunther, *Foreword: In Search of Evolving Doctrine on a Changing Court: A Model for a Newer Equal Protection,* 86 HARV. L. REV. 1, 34 (1972).

9. *Davis,* 426 U.S. at 246.

10. *Id.* at 248.

11. 429 U.S. 252 (1977).

12. *Id.* at 269.

13. *Id.* at 269–70.

14. This list is not exhaustive; the Court also mentioned the historical background of the decision and its legislative or administrative history. *Id.* at 267–68. In addition, the Court noted that disparate impact alone might suffice to establish discriminatory intent, *if* the disparate pattern was not explainable on grounds other than race. *Id.* at 266.

15. Castaneda v. Partida, 430 U.S. 482, 494 (1977). This case invalidated a "key-man" system for selecting grand jury venires, in which jurors were recommended to the court by jury commissioners who were key persons in the community. See also Alexander v. Louisiana, 405 U.S. 625 (1972); Carter v. Jury Comm'n, 396 U.S. 320 (1970); Hernandez v. Texas, 347 U.S. 475 (1954).

16. Batson v. Kentucky, 476 U.S. 79, 96 (1986)(peremptory challenges permit "those to discriminate who are of a mind to discriminate," quoting Avery v. Georgia, 345 U.S. 559, 562 (1953)).

17. Daniel R. Ortiz, *The Myth of Intent in Equal Protection*, 41 STAN. L. REV. 1105, 1127 (1989)(describing Rogers v. Lodge, 458 U.S. 613 (1982)).

18. *Davis*, 426 U.S. at 253 (Stevens, J., concurring).

19. 442 U.S. 256 (1979). _ Feeney _ See p. 44

20. *Id.* at 278–79.

21. Craig v. Boren, 429 U.S. 190 (1976).

22. See Janet W. Schofield, *Causes and Consequences of the Colorblind Perspective*, in PREJUDICE, DISCRIMINATION, AND RACISM 231, 248–50 (John F. Dovidio & Samuel L. Gaertner eds., 1986) (reporting that in an integrated school with strong emphasis on a colorblind norm, many teachers failed to use biracial or multicultural materials); Charles R. Lawrence III, *The Id, the Ego, and Equal Protection: Reckoning with Unconscious Racism*, 39 STAN. L. REV. 317, 335 (1987)(as overtly racist attitudes become culturally unacceptable, the individual must "repress or disguise racist ideas when they seek expression").

23. See, e.g., Jack Citrin et al., *White Reactions to Black Candidates: When Does Race Matter?* 54 PUB. OPINION Q. 74 (1990) ("[R]acial attitudes were a significant influence on the voting decisions of whites . . . ."); Nicholas P. Lovrich, Jr., et al., *The Racial Factor in*

Nonpartisan Judicial Elections: A Research Note, 41 W. POL. Q. 807 (1988) ("[R]ace is important in judicial elections . . . ."). But see Jane A. Piliavin, *Age, Race, and Sex Similarity to Candidates and Voting Preference,* J. APPLIED SOC. PSYCHOL. 351, 366 (1987) ("[A]geism is . . . a far stronger effect than either racism or sexism.")

24. See Nyla R. Branscombe & Eliot R. Smith, *Gender and Racial Stereotypes in Impression Formation and Social Decision-Making Processes,* 22 SEX ROLES 627, 645 (1990) ("Our results also suggest that stereotypes may have an impact by shaping the criteria used to reach decisions. With minority candidates, more confidence may be desired in order to make a decision, leading to solicitation of additional information."); William G. Doerner et al., *An Analysis of Rater-Ratee Race and Sex Influences upon Field Training Officer Program Evaluations,* 17 J. CRIM. JUST. 103 (1989) (reporting ratee race effects observed in earlier phases of training program; later diminution of effects may be attributed to attrition); Kurt Kraiger & J. Kevin Ford, *A Meta-Analysis of Ratee Race Effects in Performance Ratings,* 70 J. APPLIED PSYCHOL. 56 (1985) (stating that race effects decline as percentage of blacks in workgroup increases); Kathryn M. Neckerman & Joleen Kirschenman, *Hiring Strategies, Racial Bias, and Inner-City Workers,* 38 SOC. PROBS. 433, 445 (1991) ("Our evidence suggests that negative preconceptions and strained race relations both hamper inner-city black workers in the labor market."); David A. Waldman & Bruce J. Avolio, *Race Effects in Performance Evaluations: Controlling for Ability, Education, and Experience,* 76 J. APPLIED PSYCHOL. 897, 899 (1991) ("Results confirmed our prediction that race effects would be obtained for ratee race . . . .").

25. See Glenn B. Canner et al., *Race, Default Risk and Mortgage Lending: A Study of the FHA and Conventional Loan Markets,* 58 S. ECON. J. 249, 251 (1991) ("[A]fter controlling for household and locational default risk, findings further suggest that minority households are somewhat less likely to obtain conventional financing than whites."); Gregory D. Squires & William Velez, *Insurance Redlining and the Transformation of an Urban Metropolis,* 23 URB. AFF. Q. 63, 63 (1987) ("In analyzing the distribution of homeowners insurance

policies, a strong bias in favor of suburban and white neighborhoods and against inner-city and minority communities was found.").

26. See Harold W. Neighbors et al., *The Influence of Racial Factors on Psychiatric Diagnosis: A Review and Suggestions for Research*, 25 COMMUNITY MENTAL HEALTH J. 301 (1989) (discussing two different and inconsistent assumptions underlying research on observed race differences in psychiatric diagnosis).

27. See Charles F. Bond, Jr., et al., *Responses to Violence in a Psychiatric Setting: The Role of Patient's Race*, 14 PERSONALITY & SOC. PSYCHOL. BULL. 448 (1988) (reporting that white hospital staff restrained violent nonwhite patients four times as often as similarly violent whites).

28. See Douglas A. Smith et al., *Equity and Discretionary Justice: The Influence of Race on Police Arrest Decisions*, 75 J. CRIM. L. & CRIMINOLOGY 234 (1984) (stating that police are more responsive to white victims of crime).

29. See Cassia Spohn et al., *The Impact of the Ethnicity and Gender of Defendants on the Decision to Reject or Dismiss Felony Charges*, 25 CRIMINOLOGY 175, 175 (1987) ("Hispanic males are most likely to be prosecuted fully, followed by black males, Anglo males, and females of all ethnic groups.").

30. See George S. Bridges & Robert D. Crutchfield, *Law, Social Standing and Racial Disparities in Imprisonment*, 66 SOC. FORCES 699, 699 (1988) ("Blacks are more likely than whites to be imprisoned in states where the black population is a small percentage of the total population and predominantly urban.").

31. Each of the following studies found significant racial disparities in capital sentencing; all found that imposition of the death penalty was more likely if the victim was white, and some also found it more likely if the offender was black: David C. Baldus et al., *Comparative Review of Death Sentences: An Empirical Study of the Georgia Experience*, 74 J. CRIM. L. & CRIMINOLOGY 661 (1983); Sheldon Ekland-Olson, *Structured Discretion, Racial Bias, and the Death Penalty: The First Decade after* Furman *in Texas*, 69 SOC. SCI. Q. 853 (1988); Thomas J. Keil & Gennaro F. Vito, *Race, Homicide Severity, and*

Application of the Death Penalty: A Consideration of the Barnett Scale, 27 CRIMINOLOGY 511 (1989) (Kentucky); M. Dwayne Smith, *Patterns of Discrimination in Assessments of the Death Penalty: The Case of Louisiana,* 15 J. CRIM. JUST. 279 (1987).

Additional literature examining the effect of race on discretionary decisionmaking in the criminal process is collected and discussed in Sheri Lynn Johnson, *Black Innocence and the White Jury,* 83 MICH. L. REV. 1611 (1985); Sheri Lynn Johnson, *Race and the Decision to Detain a Suspect,* 93 YALE L.J. 214 (1983); Sheri Lynn Johnson, *Unconscious Racism and the Criminal Law,* 73 CORNELL L. REV. 1016 (1988).

32. MODEL PENAL CODE § 2.02 (1985).

33. See, e.g., W. PAGE KEETON ET AL., PROSSER AND KEETON ON THE LAW OF TORTS § 56 (5th ed. 1984) (commenting that the law's refusal to impose an obligation to go to the aid of another who is in danger is "revolting to any moral sense").

34. See Daniels v. Williams, 474 U.S. 327, 328 (1986) (holding that "the Due Process Clause is simply not implicated" by negligent deprivations of property or liberty); Davidson v. Cannon, 474 U.S. 344, 347 (1986); Estelle v. Gamble, 429 U.S. 97, 104–06 (1976) ("deliberate indifference" a prerequisite for an Eighth Amendment violation). The Court has left open the possibility that "something less than intentional conduct, such as recklessness or 'gross negligence,' is enough to trigger the protections of the Due Process Clause." *Daniels,* 474 U.S. at 334 n.3.

35. See Arizona v. Youngblood, 488 U.S. 51, 58 (1988) ("[U]nless a criminal defendant can show bad faith on the part of the police, failure to preserve potentially useful evidence does not constitute a denial of due process of law."); United States v. Leon, 468 U.S. 897 (1984); Massachusetts v. Sheppard, 468 U.S. 981 (1984) (holding that evidence obtained in reasonable reliance on a search warrant subsequently determined to be invalid should not be excluded).

36. Section 1983 provides:

Every person who, under color of any statute, ordinance, regulation, custom, or usage, of any State or Territory or the District of Columbia, subjects, or causes to be subjected, any citizen of the

United States or other person within the jurisdiction thereof to the deprivation of any rights, privileges, or immunities secured by the Constitution and laws, shall be liable to the party injured in an action at law, suit in equity, or other proper proceeding for redress. 42 U.S.C. § 1983 (1988).

37. Bivens v. Six Unknown Named Agents of the Fed. Bureau of Narcotics, 403 U.S. 388 (1971) (creating a cause of action analogous to § 1983 claims applicable to federal officials).

38. See Harlow v. Fitzgerald, 457 U.S. 800, 818 (1982) (holding that immunity is to be granted unless a federal official "violate[d] clearly established . . . constitutional rights of which a reasonable person would have known"). Though the qualified immunity doctrine is not itself a constitutional rule, it affects de facto whether the individual will be held liable for a constitutional violation.

39. See, e.g., DAVID C. BALDUS & JAMES W. L. COLE, STATISTICAL PROOF OF DISCRIMINATION (1980); STATISTICAL METHODS IN DISCRIMINATION LITIGATION 69–209 (David H. Kaye & Mikel Aickin eds., 1986).

40. 888 F.2d 591 (9th Cir. 1989).

41. This point, along with an insightful analysis of several other aspects of the *Fragante* case, can be found in Mari J. Matsuda, *Voices of America: Accent, Antidiscrimination Law, and a Jurisprudence for the Last Reconstruction*, 100 YALE L.J. 1329 (1991).

42. Frontiero v. Richardson, 411 U.S. 677, 690 (1973) (plurality opinion).

43. See William R. Van Riper, *General American: An Ambiguity*, in DIALECT AND LANGUAGE VARIATION 123 (Harold B. Allen & Michael D. Linn eds., 1986).

44. It is described in J. L. DILLARD, BLACK ENGLISH: ITS HISTORY AND USAGE IN THE UNITED STATES (1972); GENEVA SMITHERMAN, TALKIN AND TESTIFYIN: THE LANGUAGE OF BLACK AMERICA (1977).

45. *Davis*, 426 U.S. at 246.

46. Historically, education has been the centerpiece of the movement to professionalize the police. George D. Eastman & James A. McCain, *Education, Professionalism, and Law Enforcement in Histori-*

cal Perspective, 9 J. POLICE SCI. & ADMIN. 119 (1981). Differing views exist regarding the relation between higher education and police work. Compare, e.g., Daniel J. Bell, *The Police Role and Higher Education*, 7 J. POLICE SCI. & ADMIN. 467 (1979) (approving criminal justice programs in colleges and universities) and Roy R. Roberg, *An Analysis of the Relationships among Higher Education, Belief Systems, and Job Performance of Patrol Officers*, 6 J. POLICE SCI. & ADMIN. 336 (1978) (arguing that higher education fosters less dogmatic belief systems, which improve job performance) with Lotte E. Feinberg & Arthur S. Pfeffer, *"EOTWY" Meets Plain English: A Case Study of Writing in the NYPD*, 10 J. POLICE SCI. & ADMIN. 101 (1982) (arguing that liberal arts writing styles are not suited to police needs) and Jon Miller & Lincoln Fry, *Reexamining Assumptions about Education and Professionalism in Law Enforcement*, 4 J. POLICE SCI. & ADMIN. 187 (1976) (questioning whether education can increase police professionalism). In the context of the *Davis* hypothetical, Test 21 might be viewed as a proxy for educational attainment.

47. *Davis,* 512 F.2d at 966 (Robb, J., dissenting).

48. See Trina Grillo & Stephanie M. Wildman, *Obscuring the Importance of Race: The Implication of Making Comparisons between Racism and Sexism (Or Other-Isms)*, 1991 DUKE L.J. 397, 401–08 (discussing problem of whites who want people of color to teach them about racism).

NOTES TO CHAPTER 4

1. City of Richmond v. J.A. Croson Co., 488 U.S. 469, 521 (1989) (Scalia, J., concurring) (quoting ALEXANDER M. BICKEL, THE MORALITY OF CONSENT 133 (1975)).

2. See Eric Schnapper, *Affirmative Action and the Legislative History of the Fourteenth Amendment*, 71 VA. L. REV. 753 (1985).

3. Laurence H. Tribe, *"In What Vision of the Constitution Must the Law Be Color-blind?"* 20 J. MARSHALL L. REV. 201, 204 n.19 (1986) (attributing this point to the Brief of the United States as Amicus Curiae Supporting Petitioners at 14–15, Wygant v. Jackson Bd. of

Educ., 476 U.S. 267 (1986)). The argument set forth in this paragraph generally follows that made by Tribe, *supra.*

4. See Alexander M. Bickel, *The Original Understanding and the Segregation Decision,* 69 HARV. L. REV. 1, 58 (1955). An earlier work by Frank and Munro reached a similar conclusion but stated the point less conclusively. See John P. Frank & Robert F. Munro, *The Original Understanding of "Equal Protection of the Laws,"* 50 COLUM. L. REV. 131, 167–68 (1950) (expressing reservations about the conclusion that the framers intended to prohibit segregated schools and describing evidence on question of miscegenation as unclear). Several prominent scholars who, like Bickel, are strong proponents of the colorblindness principle also concede that it cannot be located in the framers' intent. See, e.g., Robert H. Bork, *Neutral Principles and Some First Amendment Problems,* 47 IND. L.J. 1, 14 (1971); Richard A. Posner, *The DeFunis Case and the Constitutionality of Preferential Treatment of Racial Minorities,* 1974 SUP. CT. REV. 1, 21–22; William Van Alstyne, *Rites of Passage: Race, the Supreme Court, and the Constitution,* 46 U. CHI. L. REV. 775, 776 (1979).

5. Bickel, *supra* note 4, at 63.

6. Of course, Justice Harlan articulated a colorblindness principle in Plessy v. Ferguson, 163 U.S. 537 (1896), but he stated the proposition in dissent. See 163 U.S. at 559 (Harlan, J., dissenting).

7. 347 U.S. 483 (1954). The leading exponents of the view that Brown did not enact colorblindness were PAUL G. KAUPER, FRONTIERS OF CONSTITUTIONAL LIBERTY 217–19 (1956) ("This decision admitted of a variety of interpretations."), Charles L. Black, Jr., *The Lawfulness of the Segregation Decisions,* 69 YALE L.J. 421, 426 (1960) (prohibition of segregation supportable on ground that it disadvantaged black children), and Herbert Wechsler, *Toward Neutral Principles of Constitutional Law,* 73 HARV. L. REV. 1, 32 (1959) ("The Court did not declare . . . that the fourteenth amendment forbids all racial lines in legislation."). But see, e.g., ALBERT P. BLAUSTEIN & CLARENCE C. FERGUSON, JR., DESEGREGATION AND THE LAW: THE MEANING AND EFFECT OF THE SCHOOL SEGREGATION CASES 145 (1957) (concluding that the Court had "declared that all classification by race is unconstitutional per se").

8. Gayle v. Browder, 352 U.S. 903, *affg. per curiam* 142 F. Supp. 707 (M.D. Ala. 1956) (three-judge court) (buses); Holmes v. City of Atlanta, 350 U.S. 879 (1955), *vacating per curiam* 223 F.2d 93 (5th Cir. 1955), *overruled by* McDermott Intl. Inc. v. Wilander, 498 U.S. 337 (1991) (municipal golf courses); Mayor of Baltimore v. Dawson, 350 U.S. 877, *affg. per curiam* 220 F.2d 386 (4th Cir. 1955) (public beaches and bathhouses).

The argument that the *per curiam* decisions compel the inference that *Brown* rested on colorblindness is set forth in some detail in Andreas Auer, *Public School Desegregation and the Color-Blind Constitution*, 27 Sw. L.J. 454, 458–59 (1973).

9. See, e.g., Swann v. Charlotte-Mecklenburg Bd. of Educ., 402 U.S. 1, 16 (1971); Auer, *supra* note 8, at 468–77 (stating that Court failed to clarify extent of government responsibility for de facto segregation); Alan D. Freeman, *Legitimizing Racial Discrimination Through Antidiscrimination Law: A Critical Review of Supreme Court Doctrine*, 62 MINN. L. REV. 1049, 1099–102 (1978) (describing "era of contradiction," in which the Court retained formal adherence to the "perpetrator" perspective while achieving results more consistent with the "victim" perspective).

10. See DeFunis v. Odegaard, 416 U.S. 312 (1974) (dismissed as moot).

11. See Regents of the Univ. of Cal. v. Bakke, 438 U.S. 265 (1978) (no majority on constitutional standard). Even absent a majority opinion, *Bakke* was the landmark case on affirmative action for several years. The Court was at least equally badly divided in five other cases that preceded and followed *Bakke*. See United Jewish Orgs. v. Carey, 430 U.S. 144 (1977) (fragmented 7–1 decision); Fullilove v. Klutznick, 448 U.S. 448 (1980) (6–3 decision; two three-member pluralities); Wygant v. Jackson Bd. of Educ., 476 U.S. 267 (1986) (5-4 decision; only four Justices specifying level of review); Local 28, Sheet Metal Workers Intl. Assn. v. EEOC, 478 U.S. 421 (1986) (on constitutional issue, five Justices finding no violation, four without specifying level of review; remaining Justices not reaching constitutional question); United States v. Paradise, 480 U.S. 149 (1987) (5-4 decision; no specification of standard of review).

12. City of Richmond v. J.A. Croson Co., 488 U.S. 469 (1989).

13. Wechsler, *supra* note 7, at 31–34. For a description of the process difficulties of *Brown*, see Gary Peller, Neutral Principles *in the 1950's,* 21 U. MICH. J. L. REF. 561 (1988). Commentators who understood colorblindness as a neutral solution to Wechsler's puzzle include Bork, *supra* note 4, at 14–15, and Louis H. Pollak, *Racial Discrimination and Judicial Integrity: A Reply to Professor Wechsler,* 108 U. PA. L. REV. 1 (1959). The collegial tone of the discussion is exemplified by Charles Black's comment that Pollak's colorblindness interpretation, which was markedly distinct from Black's own approach, seemed to him "a sound alternative ground for the desegregation holdings." Black, *supra* note 7, at 421 n.2.

14. John H. Ely, *The Constitutionality of Reverse Racial Discrimination,* 41 U. CHI. L. REV. 723, 727 (1974).

15. Opponents of affirmative action who rely, at least in part, on instrumental rationales include Morris B. Abram, *Affirmative Action: Fair Shakers and Social Engineers,* 99 HARV. L. REV. 1312, 1321–22 (1986) (arguing that affirmative action leads to political struggle and stigmatizes beneficiaries); Posner, *supra* note 4, at 12 (arguing that affirmative action encourages bigotry); William B. Reynolds, *Individualism v. Group Rights: The Legacy of* Brown, 93 YALE L.J. 995, 1002–03 (1984) (arguing that mandatory busing harms public education); Antonin Scalia, *The Disease as Cure: "In Order to Get Beyond Racism, We Must First Take Account of Race,"* 79 WASH. U. L.Q. 147, 149 (1979) (arguing that affirmative action will require hiring less qualified persons); Van Alstyne, *supra* note 4, at 808 (arguing that affirmative action exacerbates racial tensions).

16. See Frances L. Ansley, *Stirring the Ashes: Race, Class, and the Future of Civil Rights Scholarship,* 74 CORNELL L. REV. 993, 1005–23 (1989) (describing change in tone of discourse and analyzing the concept of the "innocent" white affirmative action "victim"); Thomas Ross, *Innocence and Affirmative Action,* 43 VAND. L. REV. 297 (1990) (exploring the connection between the rhetoric of innocence and racism).

17. "I have a dream that my four little children one day will live in a nation where they will not be judged by the color of their skin, but

by the content of their character." CORETTA SCOTT KING, MY LIFE
WITH MARTIN LUTHER KING, JR. 239 (1969) (quoting Martin Luther
King, Jr., Aug. 28, 1963).

18. See Janet E. Helms, *An Overview of Black Racial Identity
Theory,* in BLACK AND WHITE RACIAL IDENTITY 9 (Janet E. Helms ed.,
1990).

19. See GILBERT T. STEPHENSON, RACE DISTINCTIONS IN AMERICAN
LAW 348 (1910) (nearly every state and territory had some race-specific
classifications). For a description of the pre–Civil War attitudes of
white Americans toward blacks, see WINTHROP D. JORDAN, WHITE
OVER BLACK: AMERICAN ATTITUDES TOWARD THE NEGRO, 1550–1812
(1968).

20. Gary Peller, *Race Consciousness,* 1990 DUKE L.J. 758, 836.

21.

What is this but declaring . . . that no discrimination shall be
made against [blacks] because of their color? The words of the
amendment, it is true, are prohibitory, but they contain a necessary implication of a positive immunity, or right, most valuable
to the colored race,—the right to exemption from unfriendly
legislation against them distinctively as colored,—exemption
from legal discriminations, implying inferiority in civil society,
lessening the security of their enjoyment of the rights which
others enjoy, and discriminations which are steps toward reduc-
ing them to the condition of a subject race. Strauder v. West
Virginia, 100 U.S. 303, 307–08 (1879).

22. See sources cited in chapter 2, notes 8–13.

23. LAURENCE H. TRIBE, AMERICAN CONSTITUTIONAL LAW 567 &
n.2 (2d ed. 1988). Tribe notes, however, that an even greater number
of regulations survived review during this period. *Id.*; see also Morton
J. Horwitz, *History and Theory,* 96 YALE L.J. 1825, 1827 (1987)
(pointing out that the substantive premises of the *Lochner* era were
entirely consistent with earlier constitutional ideology).

For overviews of this period, see PAUL L. MURPHY, THE CONSTITU-
TION IN CRISIS TIMES 1918–1969, at 41–67 (1972); BENJAMIN F.
WRIGHT, THE GROWTH OF AMERICAN CONSTITUTIONAL LAW 153–70
(1942).

24. During 1935 and 1936, the Court announced eleven decisions in which crucial federal legislative provisions were held unconstitutional. Wright, *supra* note 23, at 180–82 & nn. 1–13. In 1937 President Roosevelt proposed to Congress a "Court-packing" plan that would have added to the total number of Justices on the Supreme Court one additional Justice for each sitting Justice who had reached the age of 70, ostensibly on the ground that the older Justices were unable to keep up with the Court's workload. The plan was generally understood to be designed to create a Court majority who would vote to uphold Roosevelt's New Deal legislation. William E. Leuchtenburg, *The Origins of Franklin D. Roosevelt's "Court-Packing" Plan*, 1966 SUP. CT. REV. 347, 387–400.

25. Justice Roberts, who provided the fifth vote to uphold a minimum wage statute in West Coast Hotel v. Parrish, 300 U.S. 379 (1937), is often thought to have changed his views in response to the Court-packing plan. However, a memorandum written by Justice Roberts shows that an initial vote in West Coast Hotel was taken several weeks before the President's plan was announced. See Felix Frankfurter, *Mr. Justice Roberts*, 104 U. PA. L. REV. 311, 313–15 (1955).

26. By the end of 1939, President Roosevelt had nominated, and the Senate had confirmed, four new Justices: Hugo L. Black (replacing Willis Van Devanter, who retired in 1937 during Congress' debate over the Court-packing plan); Stanley F. Reed (replacing George Sutherland, who retired in 1938); Felix Frankfurter (replacing Benjamin N. Cardozo, who died in 1938); and William O. Douglas (replacing Louis D. Brandeis, who retired in 1939). Roosevelt later named to the Court Justices Murphy (1940), Byrnes (1941), Jackson (1941), and Rutledge (1943), and he nominated Justice Harlan F. Stone to be Chief Justice in 1941.

27. See, e.g., Morris R. Cohen, *Property and Sovereignty*, 13 CORNELL L.Q. 8 (1927); Robert L. Hale, *Coercion and Distribution in a Supposedly Non-Coercive State*, 38 POL. SCI. Q. 470 (1923); Roscoe Pound, *Liberty of Contract*, 18 YALE L.J. 454 (1909); see also Horwitz, *supra* note 23, at 1829.

28. Horwitz, *supra* note 23, at 1829; see, e.g., Ferguson v. Skrupa, 372 U.S. 726, 728–31 (1963); Williamson v. Lee Optical of Oklahoma,

Inc., 348 U.S. 483, 488 (1955); Lochner v. New York, 198 U.S. 45, 74–76 (1905) (Holmes, J., dissenting).

29. See Cass R. Sunstein, *Lochner's Legacy,* 87 COLUM. L. REV. 873, 874 (1987).

30. James B. Thayer, *The Origin and Scope of the American Doctrine of Constitutional Law,* 7 HARV. L. REV. 129 (1893).

31. *Id.* at 144.

32. See *id.* at 152, 155–56.

33. Wallace Mendelson, *The Influence of James B. Thayer upon the Work of Holmes, Brandeis, and Frankfurter,* 31 VAND. L. REV. 71 (1978). Each of these Justices acknowledged Thayer's role. *Id.* at 73.

34. Historians have attributed this argument, and the insistence with which it was advanced, to the political influence of the Progressive movement. See MORTON J. HORWITZ, THE TRANSFORMATION OF AMERICAN LAW, 1870–1960, at 261 (1992); Murphy, *supra* note 23, at 70–82; Horwitz, *supra* note 23, at 1830. The democracy-based argument for judicial restraint also has been characterized as a response to the rise of fascism in Europe. See EDWARD A. PURCELL, JR., THE CRISIS OF DEMOCRATIC THEORY 218–31 (1973).

35. American Fed'n of Labor v. American Sash & Door Co., 335 U.S. 538, 555–56 (1949) (Frankfurter, J., concurring) (footnotes omitted).

36. ALEXANDER M. BICKEL, THE LEAST DANGEROUS BRANCH: THE SUPREME COURT AT THE BAR OF POLITICS 16–17 (1962). Bickel saw Thayer's rule of restraint as "aiming at accommodation with the theory of representative democracy," *id.* at 40, but Bickel's reading seems to be mistaken, if he means to attribute the "counter-majoritarian" argument to Thayer.

37. See, e.g., JESSE H. CHOPER, JUDICIAL REVIEW AND THE NATIONAL POLITICAL PROCESS: A FUNCTIONAL RECONSIDERATION OF THE ROLE OF THE SUPREME COURT 4–59 (1980); JOHN HART ELY, DEMOCRACY AND DISTRUST: A THEORY OF JUDICIAL REVIEW 4–7 (1980); MICHAEL J. PERRY, THE CONSTITUTION, THE COURTS, AND HUMAN RIGHTS 2–4 (1982). Of course, rights-based constitutional theories minimize or reject the importance of the "counter-majoritarian diffi-

culty." See, e.g., Paul Brest, *The Fundamental Rights Controversy: The Essential Contradictions of Normative Constitutional Scholarship*, 90 YALE L.J. 1063, 1064–65 (1981); G. EDWARD WHITE, *Chief Justice Marshall, Justice Holmes, and the Discourse of Constitutional Adjudication*, in INTERVENTION AND DETACHMENT: ESSAYS IN LEGAL HISTORY AND JURISPRUDENCE 238 (1994) (describing "Marshallian" and "Holmesian" approaches to constitutional interpretation).

38. This concern with the legitimacy of judicial review seems to recede in the context of race-specific "affirmative action." See David Chang, *Discriminatory Impact, Affirmative Action, and Innocent Victims: Judicial Conservatism or Conservative Justices?* 91 COLUM. L. REV. 790 (1991).

39. 401 U.S. 424 (1971).

40. Davis v. Washington, 512 F.2d 956, 959 (D.C. Cir. 1975), *rev'd sub nom.* Washington v. Davis, 426 U.S. 229 (1976).

41. The Court said only: "We have never held that the constitutional standard for adjudicating claims of invidious racial discrimination is identical to the standards applicable under Title VII, and we decline to do so today." *Davis*, 426 U.S. at 239.

42. Robert W. Bennett, *"Mere" Rationality in Constitutional Law: Judicial Review and Democratic Theory*, 67 CAL. L. REV. 1049, 1076 (1979).

43. See Frances L. Ansley, *Race and the Core Curriculum in Legal Education*, 79 CAL. L. REV. 1511, 1557–58 n.131 (1991); Charles R. Lawrence III, *The Id, the Ego, and Equal Protection: Reckoning with Unconscious Racism*, 39 STAN. L. REV. 317, 319–20 (1987).

44. Derrick A. Bell, Jr., Brown v. Board of Education *and the Interest-Convergence Dilemma*, 93 HARV. L. REV. 518, 522–23 (1980).

45. *Davis*, 426 U.S. at 248.

46. *Id.*

47. "There may be narrower scope for operation of the presumption of constitutionality when legislation appears on its face to be within a specific prohibition of the Constitution." United States v. Carolene Prods. Co., 304 U.S. 144, 152–53 n.4 (1938).

48. For commentary critical of the Court's preoccupation with the

problem of judicial review in the context of equal protection analysis, see Chang, *supra* note 38; Kenneth L. Karst, *The Supreme Court, 1976 Term—Foreword: Equal Citizenship under the Fourteenth Amendment*, 91 HARV. L. REV. 1, 3–4 (1977); Kenneth L. Karst & Harold W. Horowitz, *The* Bakke *Opinions and Equal Protection Doctrine*, 14 HARV. C.R.-C.L. L. REV. 7, 21–24 (1979).

49. See Alan D. Freeman, *Race and Class: The Dilemma of Liberal Reform*, 90 YALE L.J. 1880, 1895 (1981) (reviewing DERRICK A. BELL, JR., RACE, RACISM AND AMERICAN LAW (2d ed. 1980)). On the weaknesses of this vision, see Ansley, *supra* note 16, at 1048–50.

50. See Derrick A. Bell, Jr., *Racial Remediation: An Historical Perspective on Current Conditions*, 52 NOTRE DAME LAW. 5, 6 (1976) ("[W]hite self interest will prevail over black rights . . . ."). With respect to the desegregation cases, Mary Dudziak has provided historical documentation to support Bell's descriptive thesis that whites adopt antiracist measures only when self-interest so directs. See Mary L. Dudziak, *Desegregation as a Cold War Imperative*, 41 STAN. L. REV. 61 (1988).

NOTES TO CHAPTER 5

1. For discussions of differing cultural styles within the black community, see LURE AND LOATHING: ESSAYS ON RACE, IDENTITY, AND THE AMBIVALENCE OF ASSIMILATION (Gerald Early ed., 1993) (containing essays by black intellectuals and writers on black people's struggle between nationalistic and assimilationist models of collective identity); Jerome McCristal Culp, Jr., *The Michael Jackson Pill: Equality, Race, and Culture*, 92 MICH. L. REV. 2613 (1994) (imagining colloquies among professors, judges, and citizens of various political orientations on the subject of a fictional "Michael Jackson Pill," which would remove all "blackness" from black people).

2. On the many difficulties faced by blacks in the corporate world, see GEORGE DAVIS & GLEGG WATSON, BLACK LIFE IN CORPORATE AMERICA: SWIMMING IN THE MAINSTREAM (1982).

3. Title VII states in part:

It shall be an unlawful employment practice for an employer—

(1) to fail or refuse to hire or to discharge any individual, or otherwise to discriminate against any individual with respect to his compensation, terms, conditions, or privileges of employment, because of such individual's race, color, religion, sex, or national origin;

or

(2) to limit, segregate, or classify his employees or applicants for employment in any way which would deprive or tend to deprive any individual of employment opportunities or otherwise adversely affect his status as an employee, because of such individual's race, color, religion, sex, or national origin. 42 U.S.C. § 2000e-2(a) (1988).

4. 411 U.S. 792 (1973).

5. *McDonnell Douglas,* 411 U.S. at 802 (footnote omitted).

6. Texas Dep't of Community Affairs v. Burdine, 450 U.S. 248, 256 (1981). In addition, Title VII provides for a bona fide occupational qualification defense to some disparate treatment claims, but it is not available in race discrimination cases. See 42 U.S.C. § 2000e-2(e) (1988).

7. See St. Mary's Honor Ctr. v. Hicks, 509 U.S. 502, 511 (1993) (stating that the ultimate question for the trier of fact is whether the plaintiff has proved discrimination on the basis of race).

8. The reality may be more complex than my hypothetical cases, which focus on the comparison between Yvonne and Keisha, suggest. The perceptions of Yvonne's clients and colleagues that she inflated her billable hours may have been distorted; structuralists contend that misperception of tokens is not uncommon. See ROSABETH MOSS KANTER, MEN AND WOMEN OF THE CORPORATION 211, 230–37 (rev. ed. 1993). Moreover, the evidentiary foundation for a disparate treatment case is not always easy for a plaintiff to establish, because it requires showing that the individuals with whom the comparison is to be made were similar to the plaintiff in relevant respects.

9. Albemarle Paper Co. v. Moody, 422 U.S. 405, 425 (1975) (citing Griggs v. Duke Power Co., 401 U.S. 424, 430 (1971)). Disparate

impact, as well as disparate treatment, analysis may be used in cases involving subjective criteria of decision. Watson v. Fort Worth Bank & Trust, 487 U.S. 977, 990–91 (1988).

10. Pub. L. No. 102-166, 105 Stat. 1071 (codified at 42 U.S.C. § 2000e-2 (Supp. V 1993)).

11. The 1991 Act added the following provision:
An unlawful employment practice based on disparate impact is established under this title only if—(i) a complaining party demonstrates that a respondent uses a particular employment practice that causes a disparate impact on the basis of race, color, religion, sex, or national origin and the respondent fails to demonstrate that the challenged practice is job related for the position in question and consistent with business necessity; or (ii) the complaining party makes the demonstration described in subparagraph (C) with respect to an alternative employment practice and the respondent refuses to adopt such alternative employment practice. Civil Rights Act of 1991, Pub. L. No. 102-166, § 105(a), 105 Stat. 1071, 1074 (codified at 42 U.S.C. § 2000e-2(k)(1)(A) (Supp. V 1993)).

Subparagraph (C) provides: "The demonstration referred to by subparagraph (A)(ii) shall be in accordance with the law as it existed on June 4, 1989, with respect to the concept of 'alternative employment practice.' " 42 U.S.C. § 2000e-2(k)(1)(C) (Supp. V 1993).

Prior to passage of the 1991 Act there was considerable debate among scholars as to whether the disparate impact theory of liability was authorized by the statute. See, e.g., Alfred W. Blumrosen, *Strangers in Paradise:* Griggs v. Duke Power Co. *and the Concept of Employment Discrimination,* 71 MICH. L. REV. 59, 69–70 (1972); George Rutherglen, *Disparate Impact under Title VII: An Objective Theory of Discrimination,* 73 VA. L. REV. 1297, 1299–311 (1987).

12. 490 U.S. 642 (1989).

13. *Wards Cove,* 490 U.S. at 659–60. The Court also stated that disparate impact plaintiffs must identify the specific employment practice alleged to be the cause of a disparate effect, and that they may not challenge a multicomponent selection process as a whole. *Id.* at 657.

Congress modified this rule only slightly in the 1991 Act, by providing that a plaintiff may challenge a multicomponent process if she can establish that its elements "are not capable of separation for analysis." 42 U.S.C. § 2000e-2(k)(1)(B)(i).

14. Section 105 of the 1991 Act provides that a violation is established if the complaining party "demonstrates" the existence of a disparate impact and the respondent "fails to demonstrate that the challenged practice is job related for the position in question and consistent with business necessity." Civil Rights Act of 1991, § 105(a), 105 Stat. at 1074 (codified at 42 U.S.C. § 2000e-2(k)(1)(A)(i)). According to § 104, "[t]he term 'demonstrates' means meets the burdens of production and persuasion." *Id.* § 104(m), 105 Stat. at 1074 (codified at 42 U.S.C. § 2000e(m)).

15. *Wards Cove* rejected workforce stratification—overrepresentation of whites in higher job classifications and overrepresentation of nonwhites at lower levels—as a method of proving disparate impact. *Wards Cove,* 490 U.S. at 655. This aspect of *Wards Cove* was not affected by the 1991 Act.

16. See Elaine Shoben, *Defining the Relevant Population in Employment Discrimination Cases,* in STATISTICAL METHODS IN DISCRIMINATION LITIGATION 55 (D. H. Kaye & Mikel Aickin eds., 1986); Elaine W. Shoben, *Probing the Discriminatory Effects of Employee Selection Procedures with Disparate Impact Analysis Under Title VII,* 56 TEX. L. REV. 1 (1977).

17. The statute provides:
With respect to demonstrating that a particular employment practice causes a disparate impact as described in subparagraph (A)(i), the complaining party shall demonstrate that each particular challenged employment practice causes a disparate impact, except that if the complaining party can demonstrate to the court that the elements of a respondent's decisionmaking process are not capable of separation for analysis, the decisionmaking process may be analyzed as one employment practice. Civil Rights Act of 1991, Pub. L. No. 102-166, § 105(a), 105 Stat. 1071, 1074 (codified at 42 U.S.C. § 2000e-2(k)(1)(B)(i) (Supp. V 1993)).

There is an additional exception: "When a decision-making process includes particular, functionally-integrated practices which are components of the same criterion, standard, method of administration, or test, such as the height and weight requirements designed to measure strength in Dothard v. Rawlinson, 433 U.S. 321 (1977), the particular, functionally-integrated practices may be analyzed as one employment practice." 137 CONG. REC. S15,276 (daily ed. Oct. 25, 1991). The recognition that some clusters of employment practices may not be "capable of separation for analysis" represents a minor modification of the *Wards Cove* position.

18. 401 U.S. 424 (1971).

19. *Id.* at 431. The *Griggs* Court said as well that "[t]he touchstone is business necessity." *Id.* The relation between the job relatedness and business necessity requirements remains unclear.

20. Julia Lamber, *Alternatives to Challenged Employee Selection Criteria: The Significance of Nonstatistical Evidence in Disparate Impact Cases under Title VII*, 1985 WIS. L. REV. 1, 34–35.

21. Until 1991, a plaintiff's introduction of an alternative selection criterion with a less discriminatory impact was seen as a way of rebutting the defendant's claim of business necessity. See, e.g., Albemarle Paper Co. v. Moody, 422 U.S. 405, 425 (1975), quoted at text accompanying note 24. However, the 1991 Act might be read to permit a plaintiff to circumvent the business necessity issue by introducing an alternative employment practice, and even to permit the plaintiff to proceed by bringing forward a less discriminatory alternative without first showing the existence of a disparate impact at all. See 42 U.S.C. § 2000e-2(k)(1)(A) (Supp. V 1993), reproduced *supra* note 11. These readings of the Act will be explored further later in this chapter.

22. The contrast between the constitutional standard and the Title VII rule was described in chapter 3.

23. 422 U.S. 405 (1975).

24. 422 U.S. at 425 (citations omitted).

25. Connecticut v. Teal, 457 U.S. 440, 447 (1982) ("[Even if the defendant demonstrates job relatedness], the plaintiff may prevail, if he shows that the employer was using the practice as a mere pretext for

discrimination."); New York Transit Auth. v. Beazer, 440 U.S. 568, 587 (1979) ("The District Court's express finding that the rule was not motivated by racial animus forecloses any claim in rebuttal that it was merely a pretext for intentional discrimination."). In Dothard v. Rawlinson, 433 U.S. 321 (1977), the Court did not use "pretext" language and instead stated that "[i]f the employer proves that the challenged requirements are job related, the plaintiff may then show that other selection devices without a similar discriminatory effect would also 'serve the employer's legitimate interest in efficient and trustworthy workmanship.' " *Id.* at 329 (citation and internal quotation marks omitted).

26. Similar pretext language appears in Watson v. Fort Worth Bank & Trust, 487 U.S. 977, 998 (1988) (plurality opinion), and commanded a majority in Wards Cove Packing Co. v. Atonio, 490 U.S. 642, 660–61 (1989).

27. 487 U.S. 977 (1988).

28. *Id.* at 997.

29. *Wards Cove*, 490 U.S. at 659.

30. *Id.* at 670 (Stevens, J., dissenting).

31. For a much more sophisticated discussion of this problem, see David C. Baldus & James W. L. Cole, Statistical Proof of Discrimination § 9.1 (1980). Baldus and Cole suggest that statistical significance techniques can mitigate the difficulties associated with small sample size, at least in some instances, but also note that courts often are "preoccupied" with the small sample problem. *Id.* at 300 n.21; see also Ramona L. Paetzold & Steven L. Willborn, The Statistics of Discrimination: Using Statistical Evidence in Discrimination Cases 4–36 & n.114 (1994) (citations omitted). Examples of this phenomenon include Mayor of Philadelphia v. Educational Equality League, 415 U.S. 605, 621 (1974) (stating that the trial court's concern regarding the "smallness of the sample presented by the 13-member Panel was . . . well founded"); Waisome v. Port Auth., 948 F.2d 1370, 1376–77 (2d Cir. 1991); Bryant v. Wainwright, 686 F.2d 1373, 1377 (11th Cir. 1982); Eubanks v. Pickens-Bond Constr. Co., 635 F.2d 1341, 1347–48 (8th Cir. 1980).

32. The EEOC guidelines state:

A selection rate for any race, sex, or ethnic group which is less than four-fifths (4/5) (or eighty percent) of the rate for the group with the highest rate will generally be regarded by the Federal enforcement agencies as evidence of adverse impact, while a greater than four-fifths rate will generally not be regarded by Federal enforcement agencies as evidence of adverse impact. Equal Employment Opportunity Comm'n, Uniform Guidelines on Employee Selection Procedures, 29 C.F.R. pt. 1607.4(D) (1994).

33. See Paetzold & Willborn, *supra* note 31, at 5–10 to 5–11. These authors note that the problem of small sample size may be ameliorated by statistical significance techniques. *Id.* at 4–36 & n.115; see also 29 C.F.R. pt. 1607.4(D) ("Greater differences in selection rate may not constitute adverse impact where the differences are based on small numbers and are not statistically significant . . . ." (emphasis added)).

34. 457 U.S. 440 (1982).

35. 635 F.2d 188 (3d Cir. 1980).

36. *Id.* at 192 ("[N]o violation of Title VII can be grounded on the disparate impact theory without proof that the questioned policy or practice has had a disproportionate impact on the employer's workforce."). *Greyhound Lines* involved a black male with the skin condition pseudofolliculitis barbae (PFB), which predominantly affects black men and is severe enough to prevent shaving in approximately half of the group affected. The plaintiff argued that Greyhound's policy of prohibiting beards for employees in public contact positions had a negative impact on black males. The Third Circuit concluded that the plaintiff had not demonstrated an actual disparate effect at the Philadelphia terminal where he was employed. *Id.* at 191. The Eighth Circuit recently took the contrary view in another PFB case. Bradley v. Pizzaco of Neb., Inc., 926 F.2d 714, 716 (8th Cir. 1991) ("General population statistics are highly significant where there is no reason to believe the disqualifying characteristic potential job applicants possess differs markedly from the national population.").

37. 433 U.S. 321 (1977).

38. *Id.* at 330–31; see also Chambers v. Omaha Girls Club, Inc.,

834 F.2d 697, 701 (8th Cir. 1987) ("because of the significantly higher fertility rate among black females, the rule banning single pregnancies would impact black women more harshly," quoting Chambers v. Omaha Girls Club, Inc., 629 F. Supp. 925, 949 (D. Neb. 1986)).

39. Cf. Albemarle Paper Co. v. Moody, 422 U.S. 405, 433 (1975) (discussing difficulty in identifying criteria actually used by supervisors in ranking employees subjectively).

40. See, e.g., Fagan v. National Cash Register Co., 481 F.2d 1115, 1125 (D.C. Cir. 1973); see also Peter B. Bayer, *Mutable Characteristics and the Definition of Discrimination under Title VII*, 20 U.C. Davis L. Rev. 769, 771 (1987) (noting that courts have held that "Title VII simply does not prohibit discrimination linked to mutable characteristics").

41. 527 F. Supp. 229 (S.D.N.Y. 1981).

42. See Garcia v. Spun Steak Co., 998 F.2d 1480, 1487 (9th Cir. 1993), *cert. denied,* 512 U.S. 1228 (1994); Garcia v. Gloor, 618 F.2d 264, 270 (5th Cir. 1980), *cert. denied,* 449 U.S. 1113 (1981). But see Gutierrez v. Municipal Court, 838 F.2d 1031, 1039–40, 1045 (9th Cir. 1988) (affirming preliminary injunction against English-only rule in court offices), *vacated as moot,* 490 U.S. 1016 (1989).

43. The term "token" describes the percentage of nonwhites in a particular workplace, not the employer's state of mind. See Kanter, *supra* note 8, at 206–12.

44. 42 U.S.C. § 2000e-2(k)(1)(B)(i) (Supp. V 1993), reproduced *supra* note 17.

45. For example, the existence of an actual disparate distribution could be the consequence of factors as diverse as the employer's use of culturally biased, objective criteria, the differential availability of opportunities beyond the employer's control, or difficult-to-prove different treatment without discriminatory intent, stereotyping, or covert hostility.

46. I argued in chapter 1 that a policy of skepticism is preferable to the attempt to distinguish "genuinely" race-neutral criteria of decision. Nevertheless, the latter is explored here in the interest of thorough investigation.

47. See Barbara J. Flagg, *Enduring Principle: On Race, Process, and Constitutional Law,* 82 CAL. L. REV. 935, 969–76 (1994).

48. There may not be *any* white-specific negative characteristics. Qualities that occur more frequently in whites may take on positive connotations for that reason alone.

49. The same analysis would apply in the case of an unfavorable employment decision based on the existence of a characteristic possessed less frequently by whites.

50. See Ian F. Haney López, *The Social Construction of Race: Some Observations on Illusion, Fabrication, and Choice,* 29 HARV. C.R.-C.L. L. REV. 1, 46–53 (1994).

51. The plaintiff would have an opportunity to rebut the defendant's claim of business necessity by introducing an alternative practice that would have a less discriminatory impact.

52. That is, the analysis of necessity should conform more to the tone of Dothard v. Rawlinson, 433 U.S. 321, 322 n.14 (1977) (holding that challenged practice "must be shown to be necessary to safe and efficient job performance"), than to New York City Transit Authority v. Beazer, 440 U.S. 568, 587 n.31 (1979) (holding that the business necessity requirement is satisfied by showing that "goals [of safety and efficiency] are significantly served by—even if they do not require—[the defendant's] rule").

53. Thus, the foreseeable impact plaintiff has to depend on the existence of relevant sociological studies. This is analogous to Yvonne's dependence on the availability of evidence of different treatment, which can be difficult to obtain. The paper trail present in Ann Hopkins' case, for example, may have been unusual. See Price Waterhouse v. Hopkins, 490 U.S. 228, 232–35 (1989).

54. This aspect of difference is thoroughly explored in MARTHA MINOW, MAKING ALL THE DIFFERENCE: INCLUSION, EXCLUSION, AND AMERICAN LAW 173–224 (1990).

55. Like the foreseeable effects approach, this model would apply to a white plaintiff in any situation in which nonwhites predominate and have final authority over the management of the business, because by its terms Title VII applies to any discrimination because of race.

However, I think it exceptionally rare for whites to find themselves in the position just described. But see Ray v. University of Ark., 868 F. Supp. 1104 (E.D. Ark. 1994) (involving claim by sole white officer on campus police force of University of Arkansas at Pine Bluff).

56. The statutory language is reproduced *supra* at note 11.

57. In general, interpretation (B) would permit consideration of the business necessity issue in appropriate cases; interpretation (A) would require consideration of that issue. One could argue that because the statute uses "or," (B) is the better interpretation. However, the foreseeable impact model follows interpretation (A).

58. Through empirical research, Kanter identified this percentage as the upper boundary of "skewed groups," in which the dynamics of tokenism—including heightened visibility, contrast, and stereotyping—appear. See Kanter, *supra* note 8, at 206–42. Though Kanter's principal focus was on (white) women's fortunes in the workplace, she regarded her theory as applicable to racial tokenism as well. *Id.* at 207.

59. This analysis is very similar to what would take place at the business necessity stage under the foreseeable impact model.

60. Just as customer preference is not a bona fide occupational qualification under disparate treatment analysis, it should not satisfy the business necessity requirement. See Diaz v. Pan Am. World Airways, Inc., 442 F.2d 385 (5th Cir.), *cert. denied*, 404 U.S. 950 (1971); Wilson v. Southwest Airlines Co., 517 F. Supp. 292 (N.D. Tex. 1981).

61. Similarly, additional corporate support might have averted the harm and ensuing litigation in Thomas v. Digital Equip. Corp., 880 F.2d 1486 (1st Cir. 1989) (involving defendant firm that facilitated complaints by Indian male plaintiff's subordinates and failed to take remedial steps when work relationship suffered from complaints), and Lopez v. Schwan's Sales Enter., Inc., 845 F. Supp. 1440 (D. Kan. 1994) (concerning Mexican American salesman who received numerous customer complaints, arguably because of cultural style).

62. This portion of Title VII is reproduced *supra* at note 3.

63. However, the alternatives model does not implement a purely distributive conception of equality. Once a workplace has been redesigned in a pluralist manner, applicants and employees would not be

able to formulate less assimilationist employment practices because the workplace would no longer be (transparently) white. Put simply, a pluralist workplace is one in which qualified persons like Keisha, whose personal style differs significantly from whites' cultural expectations, have significant decisionmaking and policymaking authority, including authority over whites.

NOTES TO CHAPTER 6

1. Section 106 provides:
It shall be an unlawful employment practice for a respondent, in connection with the selection or referral of applicants or candidates for employment or promotion, to adjust the scores of, use different cutoff scores for, or otherwise alter the results of, employment related tests on the basis of race, color, religion, sex, or national origin. Civil Rights Act of 1991, Pub. L. No. 102-166, § 106, 105 Stat. 1071, 1075 (codified at 42 U.S.C. § 2000e-2(1) (Supp. V 1993)).

2. Section 703(j) of the 1964 Act reads:
Nothing contained in this subchapter shall be construed to require any employer . . . to grant preferential treatment to any individual or to any group because of the race, color, religion, sex, or national origin of the individual or group on account of an imbalance which may exist with respect to the total number or percentage of persons of any race, color, religion, sex, or national origin employed by any employer . . . in comparison with the total number or percentage of persons of such race, color, religion, sex, or national origin in any community, State, section, or other area, or in the available work force in any community, State, section, or other area. 42 U.S.C. § 2000e-2(j) (1988).
This provision was modified in very minor respects in 1972.

3. 401 U.S. 424 (1971).

4. *Id.* at 429–30.

5. *Id.* at 432 ("[G]ood intent or absence of discriminatory intent

does not redeem employment procedures or testing mechanisms that operate as 'built-in headwinds' for minority groups and are unrelated to measuring job capability.").

6. In § 2 of the Civil Rights Act of 1991, Congress set forth the factual findings that undergird the statute:

(1) additional remedies under Federal law are needed to deter unlawful harassment and intentional discrimination in the workplace;

(2) the decision of the Supreme Court in Wards Cove Packing Co. v. Atonio, 490 U.S. 642 (1989) has weakened the scope and effectiveness of Federal civil rights protections; and

(3) legislation is necessary to provide additional protections against unlawful discrimination in employment. Civil Rights Act of 1991, Pub. L. 102-166, § 2, 105 Stat. 1071, 1071.

The purposes of the 1991 Act were:

(1) to provide appropriate remedies for intentional discrimination and unlawful harassment in the workplace;

(2) to codify the concepts of "business necessity" and "job related" enunciated by the Supreme Court in Griggs v. Duke Power Co., 401 U.S. 424 (1971), and in the other Supreme Court decisions prior to Wards Cove Packing Co. v. Atonio, 490 U.S. 642 (1989);

(3) to confirm statutory authority and provide statutory guidance for the adjudication of disparate impact suits under title VII of the Civil Rights Act of 1964 (42 U.S.C. 2000e et seq.); and

(4) to respond to recent decisions of the Supreme Court by expanding the scope of relevant civil rights statutes in order to provide adequate protection to victims of discrimination. Civil Rights Act of 1991, Pub. L. No. 102-166, § 2(2), 105 Stat. 1071, 1071.

7. See *supra* chapter 5, note 14.

8. See 42 U.S.C. § 2000e-2(j) (1988), reproduced *supra* note 2.

9. Griggs v. Duke Power Co., 401 U.S. 424, 431 (1971) ("The touchstone is business necessity. If an employment practice which operates to exclude Negroes cannot be shown to be related to job perfor-

mance, the practice is prohibited."). This formulation leaves unclear the relationship between business necessity and job relatedness.

10. BELL HOOKS, *The Politics of Radical Black Subjectivity,* in YEARNING: RACE, GENDER, AND CULTURAL POLITICS 15, 15 (1990).

11. See Michael J. Perry, *The Disproportionate Impact Theory of Racial Discrimination,* 125 U. PA. L. REV. 540, 557–58 (1977) (identifying government's remedial obligations arising from historical injustices). Redistribution as an end in itself would conflict with capitalist values. See Frances L. Ansley, *Stirring the Ashes: Race, Class and the Future of Civil Rights Scholarship,* 74 CORNELL L. REV. 993, 1031–35 (1989) (discussing the tension between affirmative action's methods and an "anti-redistributionist" ideology that is prevalent in the United States).

12. As of 1991, 13 percent of white households but only 4 percent of black households held a financial interest in a business or profession; the median value of such assets was $10,352 for whites and $3,444 for blacks. U.S. BUREAU OF THE CENSUS, STATISTICAL ABSTRACT OF THE UNITED STATES: 1994, at 482 (1994).

13. The essentials of the classic debate regarding the creation of the disparate impact doctrine in *Griggs* appear in Michael Evan Gold, Griggs' *Folly: An Essay on the Theory, Problems, and Origin of the Adverse Impact Definition of Employment Discrimination and a Recommendation for Reform,* 7 INDUS. REL. L.J. 429 (1985); Katherine J. Thomson, *The Disparate Impact Theory: Congressional Intent in 1972—A Response to Gold,* 8 INDUS. REL. L.J. 105 (1986); Michael Evan Gold, *Reply to Thomson,* 8 INDUS. REL. L.J. 117 (1986); and Alfred W. Blumrosen, Griggs *Was Correctly Decided—A Response to Gold,* 8 INDUS. REL. L.J. 443 (1986).

14. See chapter 4.

15. The interpretive strategy employed here most closely resembles that proposed by Hart and Sacks. See HENRY M. HART, JR. & ALBERT M. SACKS, THE LEGAL PROCESS: BASIC PROBLEMS IN THE MAKING AND APPLICATION OF LAW 1374–80 (William N. Eskridge & Philip P. Frickey eds., 1994).

NOTES TO CHAPTER 7

1. See Charles R. Lawrence III, *The Id, the Ego, and Equal Protection: Reckoning with Unconscious Racism,* 39 STAN. L. REV. 317, 335 (1987). See also sources cited in chapter 2, notes 20 and 23.

2. See Katharine T. Bartlett & Jean O'Barr, *The Chilly Climate on College Campuses: An Expansion of the "Hate Speech" Debate,* 1990 DUKE L.J. 574, 583.

3. JOYCE TREBILCOT, TAKING RESPONSIBILITY FOR SEXUALITY 2 (1983).

4. See Joan B. Karp, *The Emotional Impact and a Model for Changing Racist Attitudes,* in IMPACTS OF RACISM ON WHITE AMERICANS 87, 89 (Benjamin P. Bowser & Raymond G. Hunt, eds., 1981).

5. For an overview of the indeterminacy thesis, see John Hasnas, *Back to the Future: From Critical Legal Studies Forward to Legal Realism, or How Not to Miss the Point of the Indeterminacy Argument,* 45 DUKE L.J. 84 (1995).

6. See chapter 3.

7. See chapter 5.

8. See, e.g., Mark Tushnet, *An Essay on Rights,* 62 TEX. L. REV. 1363 (1984).

9. WEBSTER'S THIRD NEW INTERNATIONAL DICTIONARY OF THE ENGLISH LANGUAGE, UNABRIDGED 1815 (1986).

10. See, e.g., R. M. Hare, *The Promising Game,* in THEORIES OF ETHICS 115, 124–25 (Philippa Foot ed., 1967).

11. Peggy McIntosh, *White Privilege and Male Privilege: A Personal Account of Coming to See Correspondences Through Work in Women's Studies* 2 (Wellesley College Center for Research on Women, Working Paper No. 189, 1988).

12. See Martha R. Mahoney, *Segregation, Whiteness, and Transformation,* 143 U. PA. L. REV. 1659, 1665–66 (1995).

13. See IAN F. HANEY LÓPEZ, WHITE BY LAW: THE LEGAL CONSTRUCTION OF RACE 172 (1996).

14. See *id.* at 183–90.

15. Mari J. Matsuda, *Looking to the Bottom: Critical Legal Studies and Reparations*, 22 HARV. C.R.-C.L. L. REV. 323 (1987). Note that there's a slight disanalogy here: The notion of promising is intended to provide a standard against which to measure specific doctrines; it's not a doctrinal proposal per se.

Index

About the Author

Barbara Flagg is a Professor of Law at Washington University School of Law in St. Louis. She received her J.D. degree from Boalt Hall School of Law at the University of California, Berkeley, in 1987, and her bachelor's degree from the University of California, Riverside, in 1967. She spent the intervening years following a wandering vocational path that included the Peace Corps, photographic printing, bicycle repair, philosophy, and stereo sales and repair.

After law school, Flagg served as law clerk to then–Court of Appeals Judge Ruth Bader Ginsburg, and joined the Washington University faculty the following year. She teaches constitutional law and critical jurisprudence. Her published work addresses issues of white identity and law, constitutional discourse, and essentialism.